STUDIES IN MANAGEMENT

EDITED BY

ANDREW ROBERTSON

National Institute of Economic and Social Research
Senior Research Fellow, University of Sussex
Formerly British Institute of Management

No. 4

THE NUMERATE MANAGER

FRED KEAY

Assistant Director of Studies
Ashridge Management College

THE
NUMERATE MANAGER

London

GEORGE ALLEN & UNWIN LTD

RUSKIN HOUSE . MUSEUM STREET

PRINTED IN GREAT BRITAIN
in 10 *on* 12 *pt Times type*
BY WILLMER BROTHERS LIMITED
BIRKENHEAD

CONTENTS

INTRODUCTION

THE date when the preparations for this book began can be stated exactly. On Tuesday, June 21, 1949, *The Times* carried an item announcing that the National Institute of Economic and Social Research had made an award 'to Mr F. Keay for his essay on "Factors Affecting Productivity in the Canning Industry".'

At that time the author both of the paper mentioned and of this book was on the staff of H. J. Heinz Co. Ltd. of '57 Varieties' fame. Amongst other duties he was concerned with the calculation of bonuses and the assembling of statistics on production and productivity. The work engendered thoughts and ideas on the measurement of productivity and certain aspects of management performance, but it could not be known whether these thoughts were of worth to any but a restricted group. The opportunity to submit a research paper to the National Institute of Social and Economic Research enabled the thinking to be crystallized, and the fact that the paper gained an award seemed to indicate that the thinking had some merit in a wider context.

There followed an appointment in the same firm as administrative assistant to the deputy managing director, Sir Frank Shires, who was at that time carrying simultaneously the responsibilities of director of manufacturing and director of sales. This provided an unparallelled view of the processes of decision-making and leadership in two sharply contrasting fields. Combining these responsibilities with the duty of secretary to the manufacturing staff committee, which met under the chairmanship of Sir Frank and included factory managers and the planning, research and development and engineering executives, enabled an insight to be gained into the obstacles in the way of arriving at joint conclusions and the success or failure that attended the decisions reached over a very wide range of problems indeed. This observation point had a further advantage, which accrued from being a non-executive link man between top management and those immediately below. Top management can never know all the real responses to its actions and orders, nor can the recipients of the orders always and completely be aware of the circumstances which preceded the actions and orders. An administrative assistant, whatever may be the disadvantages of his position for career building, if he has the confidence of both levels of management, is uniquely able to assess both the potential and the actual effectiveness of the various facets of managerial activity.

In this period also Sir Frank was president of the Food Manufacturers' Federation and chairman of the board of governors of the newly established National College of Food Technology. The author inevitably found himself involved in the work of both organizations, indirectly in the case of the Trade Association and directly, as a visiting lecturer on industrial management, in the case of the college. The first of these added breadth to his concepts of managerial processes and the second of them added depth and precision.

By 1955 computers, which had been used for some years in the scientific field, were beginning to be used in industrial and commercial fields also. The combination of an honours degree in mathematics, acquired at Edinburgh University prior to 1939, and of industrial and commercial knowledge gained since 1946 appealed to the computer industry at that juncture and the thought-provoking interest of computer development proved irresistible.

In the early days of computers one had to be a jack-of-all-trades dealing with whatever came along. Gradually, however, in the author's case the activity was concentrated into computing service work. The use of a service bureau provided for many firms an opportunity to discover how to use computers before taking the larger step of purchasing a machine. These firms had to be nursed through their transition from service work to ownership. In all this it soon became clear that there were barriers to thought and understanding that needed to be broken down before computers were likely to be used to full advantage.

Plenty of good work was being done in the development of new techniques which could be helpful to management and which might or might not require a computer for their successful application. What was lacking, however, in most cases was an understanding of how they could be properly used and of the real part that the computer could play. Gradually the realization grew that what was required was not just greater expertise in the use of new tools but a new philosophy of management and the definition of new attributes for managers.

In 1964 Ashridge Management College was seeking to increase in its courses the content due to the management sciences and to the use of computers. The author came on to the academic staff of Ashridge at the beginning of February, 1964, to lecture on those subjects, and began to examine specifically the concept of numeracy. In this he attempted to discover what a new philosophy of management might include and what new attributes modern managers might require.

The courses to which lectures were given included managers from all levels and much stimulating discussion ensued. Gradually a pattern for the integration into the processes of decision-making of new techniques and new approaches seemed to emerge. In particular, it seemed clear that the manager of the future, and probably also of today, had no option but to be numerate, and to become this he needed:

1 an understanding of the historical evolution of the need for numeracy;
2 an awareness of the tools of numeracy;
3 an appreciation in perspective of the types of problems facing managers;
4 a knowledge of the characteristics of information and methods of dealing with it;
5 views on the directions in which managers might move in the future.

The chapters of this book deal with these five requirements. They represent the distillation of thoughts and ideas that have been emerging since the paper on 'Factors Affecting Productivity in the Canning Industry' was written. All the influences mentioned in this introduction have contributed something.

The word 'numeracy' does not yet appear in any dictionary. Its definition as used in this book is:

'that attribute which enables a person to make logical deductions relating to a situation which has been viewed comprehensively and in detail, and whose elements have been measured.'

Adverse argument on the need for numeracy can proceed along two lines. The first is usually expressed in the form: 'That it is more important for the manager to know about men than about numeracy', and the second: 'That numeracy can be "purchased".'

In answer to the first doubt, it should be said that the argument in the first instance is not about the respective degrees of importance of leadership and decision-making; both are surely necessary. The most capable leadership available cannot save the day when the decision to be implemented is bad. There comes to mind Tennyson's poem *The Charge of the Light Brigade:*

> Half a league, half a league,
> Half a league onward,
> All in the valley of Death
> Rode the six hundred.
> 'Forward, the Light Brigade!
> Charge for the guns!' he said;
> Into the valley of Death
> Rode the six hundred.
>
> 'Forward, the Light Brigade!'
> Was there a man dismay'd?
> Not tho' the soldier knew
> Some one had blunder'd:
> Their's not to make reply,
> Their's not to reason why,
> Their's but to do and die:
> Into the valley of Death
> Rode the six hundred.

Nothing wrong with the leadership there; the fault lay with the decision, and knowing the men and maintaining their morale was of no avail, nor could it have been. Wrong decisions in business may not have fatal consequences in terms of human life, but they can be just as disastrous in other terms.

A decision has many facets. In reaching it, consideration has to be given to many aspects. There is the personnel aspect; there is the production aspect; there is the financial aspect; the economic aspect, and many others. In all these, expertise can be bought. Expertise can be bought, too, in the practice of measurement and calculation. But none of these expertises, including the skill of the mathematician, is numeracy. They all require to be assembled, applied to the right problem and assessed. Knowing what to do with the knowledge of the experts is the responsibility of the decision-maker. It is for this that numeracy is required. Numeracy can be bought, but if the manager buys numeracy he buys a decision-maker and, in so doing, whether he realizes it or not, he opts out of the decision-making.

If the decision-maker is content with less than the best, or can control completely all the circumstances of the situation, then he need not be numerate, for he is the master of the facts. If he is not able to control all the circumstances of the situation, he cannot be the master of the facts. Nevertheless, he does not wish to be their supine slave. 'But facts are chiels that winna ding' and, if he wishes to make them his allies, he needs numeracy.

Other than its uses in lectures given at Ashridge Management College from 1964 onwards, the only published references to the noun 'numeracy' in a business context, known to the author at the time of writing have been:

1 in a paper presented by Sir Edward Playfair to the annual conference of the Institute of Secretaries at Eastbourne in 1965;
2 in an article in *B.P. Shield*, the house journal of the British Petroleum Co. Ltd.; and
3 in a business article in the *Sunday Times*.

It is of interest to note that the parallel between 'numeracy' and 'literacy' has been drawn in various forms at Ashridge, by Sir Edward Playfair and in the *B.P. Shield*.

There have been rather more uses of the adjective 'numerate', a word which does appear in the Oxford Dictionary. These uses have nearly always been in the context of using operational research techniques, which is certainly a part of the application of numeracy. Numeracy, however, as developed in this book, is a wider concept involving comprehensiveness, detail, measurement and logic.

It would be surprising if, in a world in which change is rapid and continuous, management practices, and more importantly management philosophy, remained alone unchanged. The direction of future advance can only be dimly ascertained, but if the right choice of route is to be made it is important to look closely at the indications which appear on whatever signposts exist. This is what this book tries to do.

The book has been through many drafts. Many friends have been kind enough to comment and criticize it by invitation. The list is too long to give in full, but special mention must be made of Messrs Bernard Swann, Harry Johnson and David Faulkner. It is a very much better book because of the advice they have given. The encouragement given by Dr C. Macrae, Principal of Ashridge Management College, and by members of Allen and Unwin, the publishers, has provided what at times was a much-needed spur. The illustrations have been prepared by I. T. Morison and T. D.

Robinson to whom grateful thanks are due. Lastly, special thanks are due to Mrs Sheila Faulkner and Miss Susan Reynolds for their really gallant efforts in producing innumerable typed drafts, and to my wife for her patience in enduring the trials attendant on being married to a man struggling to prepare his first book.

CHAPTER I

NUMERACY

IF one stands in the centre of that great circle of stones at Stonehenge at midsummer dawn and looks in a particular direction, the sun will be observed rising immediately over a stone clearly placed there to mark the direction. A few seconds later, if one is standing in the right position, its first rays will fall on a stone at one's feet. It is only at that one moment of time in the year that this conjunction of events takes place.

It is not known exactly what was the form of the ritual that took place at that moment. It is known that there was a ritual. Although modern research suggests a more sophisticated purpose, it is commonly accepted that it was connected with the worship of the sun. Our ancestors who performed the ritual had observed quite correctly that the midsummer day sunrise marked the northernmost sunrise of the year. From then on the sun rose in a more southerly position, day by day, and stayed above the horizon for a shorter and shorter period of the day. To them it appeared to be leaving our shores and, since the crops of the following year depended on heat from the sun for their success, it had to be brought back. Hence the ritual to placate it.

Those midsummer dawn events are dubbed a ritual. They represent, however, the ancient form of business decision-making, primitive but complete. All the elements of decision-making are there as shown in Figure 1.

The initial observation of the phenomenon leads to analysis,

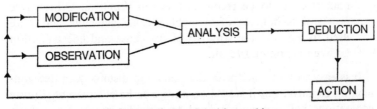

FIG. 1.—Elements of decision-making.

which in turn leads to deduction from the analysis. Action follows the deduction, which results in either the observation being repeated as before or modified in some way before the cycle is repeated.

The serious performance of this particular piece of decision-making or ritual has long been discontinued. Nobody would attempt to revive it, but it is instructive to consider why it has been discontinued.

Normally, three criteria are applied in any consideration of whether or not a business practice is to be continued, discontinued or altered. These are:

1 Are the observations accurate?
2 Is the process of analyzing the data being carried out efficiently?
3 Are the desired results of the action being achieved?

When these criteria are applied in judgement to Stonehenge decision-making, no reason emerges for discontinuing it.

First, the accuracy of the observations cannot be challenged. There are no observations used in business today that are more accurate than that of the direction of the northernmost sunrise of the year. Secondly, if speed, lack of paperwork and the minimum of people to do the processing are the hallmarks of efficiency in this context, then the operation stands comparison with any. Thirdly, the action taken was apparently remarkably successful. The sun *did* return year after year. So on these criteria there is every reason why the ancient ritual should be performed.

The truth is that, long since, in considering the Stonehenge ritual two other criteria were applied.

1 The blinkers were removed in looking at the local situation. Information acquired from other areas of human knowledge was found to be relevant to a result which had been thought to be achieved solely by the ritual itself. The action was discovered to be neither right nor wrong, but irrelevant.
2 The techniques of deduction used by the Stonehenge decision-makers came to be recognized as too primitive. Other more powerful techniques of thought became available and were used to measure the strength of the cause and effect relation between action and result.

It is easy to look back over the years and dismiss such decision-making as naïve, but it would be unwise to be complacent. Future generations will not find it hard to consider much of twentieth-century decision-making equally naïve; naïve, too, for precisely the same reasons, that it is too narrow a process and that it does not use sufficiently powerful deductive tools.

An example of how a narrow decision-making process had breadth added to it occurred in a chemical manufacturing firm. The raw material stock control procedure operated in familiar fashion by setting an ordering level for each material. When stocks fell to this ordering level, signals indicated that the appropriate ordering procedure was to be followed and purchasing requisitions were prepared. The success of this type of control procedure depends on how efficiently the records are kept up to date and on how accurately the ordering levels for each material are fixed. Record up-dating was kept at a high level of efficiency by good supervision and the matter of fixing the ordering levels correctly received periodically the attention of a conventional organization and methods department.

Simultaneously, but independently, there was a production scheduling procedure for the control of the inventory of finished goods. This operated through a mechanism which compared actual sales with estimated sales at regular intervals. Again the procedure which linked the sales variances with changes in the production schedule received the regular and careful attention of the organization and methods department.

These two systems were worked by separate staffs and in separate locations within the firm, and caused no particular concern. Eventually, in the normal course of routine investigations by the organization and methods department, both were considered as suitable for computer working and steps were taken to have them programmed for the computer at the local service bureau. Hitherto the two procedures had thrown up their operating decisions on different days of the week but, since it was desired to make a single visit to the bureau cover both operations, it was decided to synchronize the two time scales.

Now, for the first time, it came to be realized that the two procedures were not really independent. True, annual budgeting had included the calculation of a raw material budget from the accepted sales estimate. Thereafter, however, the raw materials budget was used merely to provide a financial total and the sales estimate was confined to its own local control procedure.

Yet, raw materials are required *only* to produce finished goods. The possibility of stockpiling qualifies that statement, but only to a minor and temporary extent. Variations in raw material requirements occur only because of differences between actual sales and estimated sales. The fact of the relationship between purchasing requisitions of raw materials and sales variances is obvious, although its exact nature is obscure. If its nature can be established, then one and the same procedure operating from the sales variances can control simultaneously both the production of finished goods and the purchasing of raw materials.

In the case of the chemical manufacturing firm the nature of the relationship was established. This required considerable investigation and some quite sophisticated reasoning was needed to work out the effect of time lags in changing production schedules and lead times in obtaining raw materials. Also, a formula had to be devised to avoid rapid short-term alterations which might be reversed some time later. Eventually success was achieved, and a single computer programme produced both the revisions in the production schedules and the consequential purchasing programmes.

The first principle of numeracy had been applied. This is that the approach to providing solutions to problems should be a broad one. The second principle, namely that the decision-making should be quantitative rather than qualitative, was also applied and, in the applying, Kipling's example to decision-makers correctly assessed as stopping short of what is necessary.

> I keep six honest serving-men
> (They taught me all I knew);
> Their names are What and Why and When
> And How and Where and Who.

To this the numerate manager adds 'How Much'.

Completely quantitative decision-making is sometimes not possible for a variety of reasons. Often, however, qualitative decision-making takes the form of no decision at all, when the injection of measurement might have led to one.

At one extreme this is due to inertia. A story has been told, in illustration of this, of and by the present chairman of a British company, who before the Second World War was a member of His Majesty's Government. Taking over the room allotted to him in one of his earlier ministerial appointments he sat at his desk and looked through his papers. As he did so he became conscious of a measured tread in the corridor outside his door. After a time he quietly opened the door and peeped out, and saw to his surprise a member of one of the Services on sentry duty outside his door. He continued to be there during normal working hours, day after day. To his later enquiry as to why this was so, nobody could at first give the answer. Probing, however, eventually brought an explanation of the reason, which went back some one hundred and thirty years to the time of the Prince Regent. The Prince Regent had occupied that self-same room and had been provided with a private lavatory for his own use. The sentry was there to prevent anybody else using it. The Prince Regent had gone, the lavatory had gone, but the sentry was still there!

On the other hand, qualitative decision-making may be as a result of dynamic leadership. Dynamic leadership was certainly what the founder of the H. J. Heinz Company possessed in full measure. The story of how the American firm grew from the original picking, grating and packing of horseradish in his mother's kitchen is a well-known one. Not so well known is the story of the early days of the British side of the business.

The story of the British house of Heinz began in 1886, seventeen years after the founding of the American firm. In that year Henry J. Heinz came to Europe, partly in order to visit Germany, the home of his ancestors, and partly with the definite plan of establishing the name of Heinz in Britain. He took up his abode in London and, looking around, quickly identified Fortnum and Mason's in Piccadilly as a well-thought-of store. To recognize was to act and he promptly mounted his campaign. He determined that he personally would call on the most important member of Fortnum and Mason's.

He did so, and such was the power of his persuasion, the excellence of the product he had come to sell and the vigour of his personality, that success was immediate. Henry J. Heinz returned to his hotel in triumph, well pleased with himself and with very good reason. He had done an excellent job of dynamic selling.

Nevertheless his decision that day to visit Fortnum and Mason's, though it seemed successful on the surface, was not to bring success. Not until 1919, the year in which the founder of the business died, was the British Heinz to make a profit.

The reasons for this were two-fold. In the first place, the lines which Fortnum and Mason's were prepared to stock were not the big-selling plebeian lines. Euchred figs, stem ginger and so on could not produce sufficient profit to expand a business operating initially from a base three thousand miles away. On the other hand, the suburban grocer, who might have sold his customers the profitable lines like baked beans, largely wrote Heinz off as catering only for the aristocracy. A lot of time and hard work was needed before this prejudice could be overcome.

Now although qualitative decisions are not necessarily wrong or inappropriate, here was a case where dynamic leadership led to a qualitative decision that was wrong, and where a quantitative approach was possible and should have been used.

Stephen Potter, in his history of Heinz in Britain called *The Magic Number*, asks this question: 'Would he [Henry J. Heinz] have been depressed if he had known that for twenty years this little trickle of "57" he had started was never to grow much larger—that indeed the tap was never to be turned full on for nearly twenty years after that?' He goes on to comment, 'On the whole it would have pleased him. It was perfectly in line with his theory of the pilot scheme'.

Certainly, without numeracy, there may be little alternative for the wise manager. However, there are disadvantages about basing decisions on pilot schemes. On the one hand, they are both costly to mount, they tie up resources and, on the other hand, the conclusions derived from an exercise on a small scale may not be valid when the operation becomes large-scale. Many of the factors that are important in the large-scale operation may be absent or have little effect in the pilot scheme.

How much better if the whole complete situation can be visualized in the mind, its elements measured and reliable techniques of deduction applied to determine the logical consequences of any action taken. Can it be done? Judgement on this point should be reserved until the rest of the book has been read. The third principle of numeracy, however, is that the attempt should be made.

This type of managerial approach to decision-making is at the opposite end of the spectrum from decision-making by hunch. Probably there is no such thing as 'pure hunch'. Business acumen, which gives the appearance of hunch, consists of the ability to draw upon a fund of unexpressed and unorganized assessments of relevant factors. As the pace of life accelerates and its complexity increases, this becomes more difficult, if the fund remains unorganized, and once the task has to be shared with others it becomes impossible, if unexpressed. Numeracy, in applying its third principle, sets out to organize and express.

If the organization and expression are to be useful, a language must be found in which the ideas to be communicated can be handled precisely and concisely. The language of every day is neither precise enough nor concise enough. Consider, for example, the variety of meanings that would be attached by different people to the meaning of the word 'best'. Precision is absent. Or read the following account of the process of calculating the standard cost of the materials in a finished product. 'To calculate the materials standard cost of a product containing several ingredients, take the quantity of the first ingredient and multiply it by its appropriate unit cost. Do the same for each of the ingredients in turn, add together the results of the calculations and divide the total by the total quantity of the ingredients.' This may be exact, but is certainly not concise.

The language of everyday has two further defects. It is unable to communicate across a national border when different languages are to be found on either side of that border. Further, it fails to provide a means whereby a thinker in one field of knowledge can adequately convey his thought to a thinker in another field.

Fortunately there is a language in which these defects do not apply. This is the language of mathematics, using it in the widest sense to include logic. At the mention of the word mathematics the average business man, even if he is prepared to accept that his decisions should be reasoned and calculated, begins to show signs of fear.

Yet the fear of mathematics is irrational. It is based on a judgement which is qualitative and on a failure to realize that what the non-mathematician refers to as mathematics is not a mystery but a language. The power of mathematics lies in the fact that, since it expresses basic human thought processes, it is a universal language. Indeed it is the *only* universal language, international in its use and enabling those who use it, of whatever race or tongue they may be, to communicate with each other. It overcomes, too, the boundaries of mental discipline which separate, say, the engineer and the chemist, the economist and the astronomer, the accountant and the statistician, the business man and the non-business man. These things it achieves with the utmost precision and conciseness.

Consider again the accountant's definition of the process of calculating the standard cost of the materials in a finished product. 'To calculate the materials standard cost of a product containing several ingredients, take the quantity of the first ingredient and multiply it by its appropriate unit cost. Do the same for each of the ingredients in turn, add together the results of the calculations and divide the total by the total quantity of the ingredients.'

The accountant who has learnt the use of symbols will state the process in the following terms:

'If c be the materials standard cost of product, q_1, q_2, q_3 .... etc. the quantities of each ingredient and c_1, c_2, c_3 .... etc. their respective unit costs, then

$$c = (q_1 c_1 + q_2 c_2 + q_3 c_3 + + + +) \div (q_1 + q_2 + q_3 + + + +)'$$

The second description says exactly the same thing as the first, no more and no less. It says it in a different language. By using the different language the gain in conciseness is considerable.

A qualified mathematician would express the same thing in this form:

$$c = \sum_{r=1}^{n} q_r c_r \div \sum_{r=1}^{n} q_r$$

where n is the number of ingredients.

Mysterious though this may seem to the non-mathematician, it will be understood by those who know the language of mathematics as also saying no more and no less than either of the two previous descriptions. It says it in a different language. Of the three, the last is the most concise.

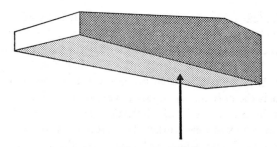

FIG. 2.—Support for horizontal beam.

There is a further point to notice. The engineer calculating the support point for a horizontal beam, in one form of the calculation would arrive at exactly the same form of expression.

$$c = \sum_{r=1}^{n} x_r c_r \div \sum_{r=1}^{n} x_r$$

The accountant calculating the standard cost of the raw material content of his finished product, and the engineer calculating the support point of a horizontal beam both arrive at the same expression. This is no accident. They arrive at the same expression because both are following exactly the same fundamental thought process. In both cases there are two series of measurements. For the accountant these measurements represent quantities of ingredients and their unit costs, while for the engineer the measurements represent the weight of different sections of the beam and their distances from one end of the beam.

Both then follow the same steps:

1 Take the first item of the first series, multiply it by the first item of the second series.
2 Take the second item of the first series, multiply it by the second item of the second series.
3 Do the same for the third items, the fourth, the fifth and so on.
4 Add together the results of these multiplications and divide by the total of one of the series.

THE POWER OF MATHEMATICAL LANGUAGE

Both the accountant and the engineer are doing precisely the same thing and therefore the mathematical expression of what each is doing is precisely the same. This is one of the powerful attributes of the language of mathematics and it makes possible the cross-fertilization of ideas from one field of human knowledge to another. Consider, for example, the medical research worker working on cancer research, the economist talking about inflation, the sales director forecasting his sales, and the engineer discussing hysteresis. On the face of it, they are all doing different things and have nothing to say to each other. Yet every one of the four is dealing with the same mathematical concept—the concept of growth or decay, which is negative growth. The medical research worker is dealing with the growth of cancer cells, the economist with the decay of the purchasing power of money, the sales director with either the growth or decay of his sales whichever is the case, and the engineer with the decay of the forces of nature. Only if they express their thoughts mathematically can they communicate with each other and find it possible to learn from each other. If they do not, then their knowledge remains local and unshared.

The use of mathematical language and the symbols appropriate to it thus provide a bridge from one discipline to another. The engineer, given the formula and the data relating to the symbols could, in this respect, do the work of the accountant and vice versa. He would not in the least require to know the significance of the symbols. A third person, moreover, neither an accountant nor an engineer, and indeed trained in no special skill at all, but qualified in mathematics, is able to go into the work of either as far as it can be identified in the form of generalized formulae and represented by symbols.

This is not to deny that there comes a stage in the work of any professional or craftsman when his own particular language, with its own terminology, has to be employed if a real understanding in depth of his own particular process is to be obtained. Before that stage is reached, however, and even in part after it, the thought processes underlying any specialized subject can be described in a form and in a language which makes it easier to apply universal rules of logical interpretation.

The fourth and fifth principles of numeracy can now be stated.

The fourth is that the fundamental thought processes occurring in different areas of human knowledge are themselves not different in kind.

The fifth is that knowledge obtained from the development of fundamental thought processes in one field of application can be communicated if it is expressed in the universal language of logic and mathematics.

RISKS OF MISINTERPRETATION

The use of any language involves the risk of falling into traps of misinterpretation for the unwary. The language of mathematics, though it has the quality of precision in greater measure than any other, is not free from this difficulty. Consider, for instance, the following situation.

A board of directors is in the throes of completing its capital spending plans for the year ahead. Appropriations already approved total £3,900,000 and it is estimated that the return on this investment will be £156,000, giving a yield of 4 per cent. There are physical resources available for one more project and there are no problems in making available the necessary financial resources. Two projects are put forward for consideration, and it happens that each of them utilizes exactly the whole of the physical resources that are available.

The details of the first of these projects is that £200,000 needs to be expended and that the return on the investment will be £26,000, giving a yield of 13 per cent. The second project requires the expenditure of £800,000 on which the return will be £79,000, giving a yield of 9·875 per cent.

There are at least three possible bases for deciding which of these two projects should be chosen to complete the capital budget. The three most commonly used are:

1 which of the projects ties up the lesser amount of capital;
2 which of the projects produces the greater amount of return in money;
3 which of the projects is the more profitable measured in terms of the percentage yield.

Since neither the level of funds available nor the amount of the cash flow is a matter of absolutely prime importance, the view is expressed at the board meeting that the criterion to be used in judging should be which of the two projects is the more profitable. Indeed, one director is heard to remark that this should always be the criterion and that he could not see what point there was in discussing any other. This then receives general acceptance, and the first project, which gives a yield of 13 per cent as against 9·875 per cent from the second, is chosen to complete the capital budget. The finance director promises to have the final figures prepared.

When the meeting is resumed after lunch, the finance director does present the final figures for the capital budget, which now comprises a total expenditure of £4,100,000 on which a return of £182,000 can be expected, giving a yield of 4·4 per cent. The board note with satisfaction that by including the project which in itself has a yield of 13 per cent the overall yield has been pushed up from 4 per cent to 4·4 per cent. This seems to be a very satisfactory conclusion.

They are about to move on to the next item of business when one director interposes that he has something further to say on the subject. He continues by remarking that he has been doing some more sums and now wonders whether they have made the right decision. Pressed, he explains that, if they had chosen the other project, the yield on the total capital budget would have gone up to 5 per cent instead of the 4·4 per cent with which they are so pleased. To the objection that this must be arrant nonsense since the yield on the second project was only 9·875 per cent compared with the

13 per cent on the first, he sticks to his guns and replies that the figures speak for themselves.

And of course he is right, as the following table clearly shows:

| | Project 1 | | | Project 2 | | |
	Capital	Return	To yield	Capital	Return	To yield
Initially	£3,900,000	£156,000	4%	£3,900,000	£156,000	4%
Project	200,000	26,000	13%	800,000	79,000	9·875%
Finally	4,100,000	182,000	4·4%	4,700,000	235,000	5%

This puts the cat amongst the pigeons and the decision is temporarily shelved. The meeting is adjourned to allow the members of the board an opportunity to consider further the significance of the figures now put forward.

Most of the members start by looking for an anomaly and, it is suspected, this is what most members of most other boards would do also. There is however no anomaly. In this particular set of circumstances it just happens to be the case that, faced with the choice of which of two unequal yields at different levels of investment to add to an existing yield the right choice is the lower of the two yields. The mistake lies in assuming that when handling ratios the rules of arithmetic should be applied in the same way, or that the same sort of results emerge in the handling of ratios as in handling absolute numbers. The example explained above is met more often perhaps in the reverse form, where a capital budget is too large and some project has to be dropped from it. The same difficulty may be experienced that, if the final yield for the budget is to be kept at its highest, the project to be abandoned is not necessarily the one with the lowest individual yield.

There is no consolation to be obtained from thinking that this is a special sort of problem only to be encountered in the making up of capital budgets. This is not the case. Ratios are one of the staples in judging performance in most walks of business life. Averages are ratios and percentages of every kind are ratios, and the same warnings need to be borne in mind when making deductions about their behaviour.

Insurance companies, for example, use as a measure of performance the expense ratio, defined as the cost of obtaining new business, expressed as a percentage of the value of business obtained. The problem stated above could be restated in insurance terms exactly as it stands or with as many zeros as one liked omitted or added.

The alteration in the number of zeros would not alter the principles so long as the ratios remained the same. Consider, then, two branches of an insurance company with identical results for eleven months of the year in value of business obtained and in the cost of obtaining it. Therefore each has the same expense ratio. In the last month of the year the two branches show figures of value of business obtained and cost of obtaining it of the same form as in the capital budget example. The same sort of result will ensue. The branch with the lower expense ratio in the final month may, nevertheless, end up with the higher expense ratio for the year, even though both had identical figures in all respects for eleven months of the year.

Or cite the example in terms of advertising appropriations, with the ratios representing numbers of the population covered per thousand pounds of expenditure in various publicity media. The principles of numeracy state that, indeed, this is the same problem as the insurance example and also the capital budget example. The change in the framework in which the example is set makes no difference and the same result necessarily follows in each case.

In the situations just described, the decision that is taken depends on whether the crucial items are looked at in isolation or as part of the whole. The form of the presentation was the same in each case. On the other hand, instances arise where the decision is influenced by the form of the presentation itself.

Consider a situation in which a company has recently taken steps to encourage its customers to increase the average size of their orders. It now wishes to review progress, and to do so examines the results of the business in the month immediately prior to the introduction of the new policy and in the month following. It so happens that twenty orders had been received during each of the months. The orders were considered to be representative and the comparison in consequence a fair one.

The accounts department listed the value of the orders as shewn in the table overleaf.

The chief accountant therefore reported that the new policy had not succeeded in increasing the average size of orders placed.

While he was doing this the sales manager, with an equal interest, was studying the figures presented to him by his own subordinates. The sales organization was divided into six regions, and each of the six regional managers had been asked to provide a statement of the average value of the orders received in his own region before and after the policy change that had been initiated. In conformity with

Value of Orders

	Before (No. of orders: 20)	*After* (No. of orders: 20)
	£11 8s	£11 12s
	11 6s	11 10s
	11 4s	11 8s
	11 2s	10 6s
	10 0s	10 4s
	10 4s	10 6s
	11 18s	10 4s
	12 0s	12 2s
	12 4s	12 4s
	12 4s	12 0s
	11 16s	12 2s
	11 18s	12 0s
	11 16s	11 0s
	11 16s	11 0s
	10 16s	10 18s
	10 14s	10 16s
	10 18s	11 2s
	10 18s	11 2s
	10 16s	11 0s
	10 14s	10 18s
Total:	£225 12s	£223 14s
Average value of order:	£11 5s 7d	£11 3s 8d

the general directive issued, these figures were to relate to the months immediately before and after the date of the change.

The six reports which reached the sales manager were based on exactly the same orders as were being scrutinized in the accounts department, and were as follows:

Value of Orders

	Before	*After*
Region A	£11 8s	£11 12s
	11 6s	11 10s
	11 4s	11 8s
	11 2s	

Average value of order before policy change   £11   5s
Average value of order after policy change   £11 10s

	Before	*After*
Region B	£10 0s	£10 6s
	10 4s	10 4s
		10 6s
		10 4s

Average value of order before policy change   £10   2s
Average value of order after policy change   £10   5s

	Before	After
Region C	£11 18s	£12 2s
	12 0s	12 4s
	12 4s	
	12 4s	

Average value of order before policy change   £12 1s 6d
Average value of order after policy change   £12 3s 0d

	Before	After
Region D	£11 16s	£12 0s
	11 18s	12 2s
	11 16s	12 0s
	11 16s	

Average value of order before policy change   £11 17s
Average value of order after policy change   £12 1s

	Before	After
Region E	£10 16s	£11 0s
	10 14s	11 0s
		10 18s
		10 16s

Average value of order before policy change   £10 15s
Average value of order after policy change   £10 18s 6d

	Before	After
Region F	£10 18s	£11 2s
	10 18s	11 2s
	10 16s	11 0s
	10 14s	10 18s

Average value of order before policy change   £10 16s 6d
Average value of order after policy change   £11 0s 6d

The sales manager noticed that in every one of his regions the average value of order had increased and therefore reported that the new policy had succeeded, thus contradicting the chief accountant who had reported the opposite.

Leaving aside any discussion on which of the two interpretations, if either, is correct, it will be seen that the form of the conclusion is dictated by the form of presentation. If one is tempted to argue that there are too few orders included to enable a reliable judgement to be formed, the exercise should be repeated, with each of the values included 100 times so that the judgement is based on 2,000 orders instead of 20. The same conclusions will emerge.

In this case there is only one set of facts to interpret, since both sets of results are the same. The manager's decision depends on which particular way the results are summarized and presented. The real power lies in the hands of the person who chooses the method of preparation of the facts. Unless he is dealing with a numerate manager, it is his form of presentation which will largely influence the nature of the decision which is taken. The facts are objective, but methods of presenting them are highly subjective, unless great care is taken in deciding what form the presentation should take.

The manager who is not sufficiently numerate runs two serious risks. He may himself actually make the wrong decision, as in the first set of examples, or he may in effect abdicate his responsibility of decision-making to the presenter of the information on which his decision is to be based, as in the second set.

The sixth and final principle of numeracy therefore is that the lack of at least an elementary knowledge of its language and syntactical rules often leads to wrong decisions or abdication of decision-making.

The vocabulary that the numerate manager acquires need not be more than is sufficient for the purpose of comprehending the lines of thought of his supporting specialists. These will include mathematicians and other operational researchers, computer specialists, financial experts, economists and organization and methods investigators. To control such a team he needs to have some familiarity with their languages.

EVOLUTION OF MANAGEMENT

Numerate decision-making is a far cry from the Stonehenge type of decision-making, but the evolution of the former from the latter can be traced. Industrial historians tell a story mainly of gradual change, growth and evolution over many centuries. Every now and then, however, there occurred a much more explosive development, to which the name revolution applies. In the early history of man the family was the only unit. Considered as an industrial unit, the family would certainly gradually change and improve its practices, but the first occasion on which one family combined with another family to achieve a common purpose created a revolutionary new situation requiring a set of relationships no longer based on the natural bonds of the family. The extension of combination with others outside the family brought into being a new element of management. This was the development of the leadership principle, the leader no longer able to rely on the ties of blood, but requiring new attributes. The leader became leader because he possessed in greater measure than anyone else, not only strength of character which may sometimes have been merely physical strength, but also an alertness in recognizing a situation and reacting to it. Even in the animal kingdom sheer size and strength has to be supported by some other attribute. Descriptions of animal behaviour give many examples. 'In the confined spaces of an aquarium a few large *Dytiscus* larvae will, within a few days, eat all living things over about a quarter of an inch long. What happens then? They will eat each other if they have not already done so; this depends less on who is bigger and stronger than upon who succeeds in seizing the other first.'

With strength of character substituted for physical strength, these attributes have continued ever since to be the marks of leadership. At that early stage of industrial organization, the only form of decision-making was that embodied in the reaction by the leader to events.

Some of the stones at Stonehenge are reputed to have been man-handled to their location on Salisbury Plain from the Prescilly Mountains in west Wales, the only place in the British Isles where stones of that type are to be found. The man who first devised a method of intertwining two or more creepers together to give added strength certainly effected an improvement in the operation of hauling stones by a single strand of creeper, but no alteration in the method of operation ensued, nor in the management practice necessary to see that the job was planned and done. On the other hand, the man who invented the wheel introduced a labour-saving device which necessitated considerable changes in the method of planning the movement of objects. Moreover, he immediately introduced a new element into leadership and decision-making. The advent of the wheel brought with it the first specialization, and the first dent in the omniscience of the leader, who found that he now had to make use of the specialist man who knew about wheels and what to do if they broke down. To the attributes of strength of character and alertness of reaction there now had to be added intelligence in resolving possible conflicts of views. These remained the attributes of the leader and decision-maker, or manager to give him his modern title, virtually until the beginning of the nineteenth century. He continued to remain in direct control of the human and physical aids at his command and in direct contact with the events of his environment.

The established order was shattered by the first industrial

revolution. This was not a revolution in the sense that the movement was short and sharp. Professor T. S. Ashton, in the Home University Library volume entitled *The Industrial Revolution*, puts the period for the movement as 1760–1830. It was, however, a revolution in the sense that a radical change was effected in the industrial scene and not merely a modification. The method by which this change came about is of importance in considering the evolution of the manager. It had several features.

CHARACTERISTICS OF THE FIRST INDUSTRIAL REVOLUTION

The inventions and developments to which the title Industrial Revolution is applied did not suddenly emerge, unconnected with events of earlier ages. They stemmed in a very direct sense from pure thinking of philosophers and scientists who lived over a century earlier. As Professor Ashton writes, 'The stream of English scientific thought, issuing from the teaching of Francis Bacon, and enlarged by the genius of Boyle and Newton, was one of the main tributaries of the industrial revolution. Newton, indeed was too good a philosopher and scholar to care whether or not the ideas he gave to the world were immediately useful, but the belief in the possibility of achieving industrial progress by the method of observation and experiment came to the eighteenth century largely through him.'

When the trickle of inventions had grown into a stream, and this in turn into the flood of the industrial revolution, one invention in particular came to be regarded as the symbol of the revolution. This was Watt's steam engine. Those whose knowledge of the events of the industrial revolution is of the scantiest would almost certainly be able to list as one of their known facts that James Watt was the inventor of the steam engine. A symbol needs a popular legend behind it, and the story of James Watt watching the kettle on the hob has that of value, although it does less than justice to the other characters in the true story.

This conclusive push of Britain into the industrial age was due in the first place to the effective harnessing of a new form of power, namely steam. This by itself was not a sufficiently powerful push. It required, in addition, to be harnessed to a new method of performing familiar tasks previously done by hand, and of extending the power of hands to undertake work hitherto beyond their scope.

The inventors, as pioneers, met with apathy and also with obstruction. Considerable time was needed before the advantages of their inventions came to be appreciated. The most beneficial of the new inventions required for their most efficient use a change in the form of industrial organization. The accepted cottage-type industry, with workers working in their own homes or in small units and a supporting servicing system organized to provide the materials and to collect the finished work, had to give way to the factory system which was the characteristic mark of nineteenth-century industry. The concentration of many workers in one location supported by a different type of servicing system—this one providing the new equipment which was too bulky and complicated to be other than centrally located—was the only type of organization which would work. This was early realized in some quarters, and first of all in Britain in the silk industry. Using machines which had been developed not in Britain but in Italy, the brothers John and Thomas Lombe in 1717 set up the first real factory, or 'manufactory' to give it its earliest name, in Derby. Also near Derby at Cromford, Arkwright, the inventor of the water frame as a means of increasing the output of spun yarn, backed by a hosiery manufacturer named Strutt, established in 1771 a similar manufactory. This new concept was greeted with much suspicion and hostility, and the growth of the factory system still lay in the middle distance.

On the other hand the inventions which were initially taken up were those which could be used without disturbing the existing forms of industrial organization. The course of events in the textile industry typifies the reactions of managements generally. In 1767 Hargreaves invented his spinning jenny, one year before Arkwright pioneered his water frame. The value of both as a means of increasing the output of spun yarn was quickly appreciated. Equally quickly the difference between the two was assessed. The jenny could be worked in the home and the water frame could not. The jenny, therefore, came into widespread use, while the water frame did not. A similar tale could be told of other inventions. A boom in the textile industry certainly developed, but it was held back by the continuing conflict between power and hand looms. Until the early part of the nineteenth century the attempt to meet the boom was made by expanding small-scale production units rather than by developing factory units.

When acceptance of the new factory system as the right type of organization became general, progress was very rapid indeed. The

c

results, by which Great Britain built for herself a dominating position in the industrial societies of the nineteenth century and became the workshop of the world, is a familiar story. There was a vacuum which needed filling, caused by the impoverishment of the continental countries as a result of the Napoleonic wars. There were markets ready for the taking, and this no doubt provided the final extra incentive.

The movement for innovation did not in general come from within the industries themselves. James Watt was originally an instrument maker. William Murdoch, who assisted in the development of the steam engine, started his working life as a country stone mason. Of the innovators in the textile industry, Richard Arkwright was a barber and John Kay a clockmaker. The recognition of the value of the inventions and the encouragement for their furthering came not from the managers of the day (who were few in number). They had in any case neither the financial means to back experiments nor the knowledge and education to be of assistance. Many of them were indeed quite illiterate. It was either the educated or the upper classes who moved the industrial revolution along.

THE NEED FOR LITERACY

The changes brought about by the industrial revolution wrought corresponding changes in the practice of management. The manager found himself dealing with larger and larger units which he could no longer handle personally. Nor could he continue to maintain direct contact with all the events that were occurring in his domain. He was forced to rely on reports of events brought to him, rather than on his observation of the events themselves. Inevitably, much of his management became indirect rather than direct. Consequently, he found that the attributes which he possessed—strength of character, alertness in recognizing situations and intelligence in deciding conflicting views, although still necessary, were no longer sufficient. He now needed the further attribute of literacy. This he had *not* needed when he could supervise directly the activities of all and when he could observe directly all the results of these activities. He needed it now, because he had to evolve a system of indirect control, supported by a method of communicating instructions in one direction and of receiving information in the other. Reliance on verbal methods would soon be found ineffective and written communication became a necessity. So for top management, and before long for lower grades of management also, literacy became a necessary attribute to be added to those that had served in the past.

The practice of management is not confined to the manufacturing industry. The observation of events, their interpretation through analysis and the deduction of the implications which they hold is just as fundamental to the regulation of events in commerce and administration, both public and private. In all these fields the touchstone of whether literacy is a necessary attribute for the manager, director or administrator at any level is whether he is in a position to react directly to the events themselves, or whether he is compelled to react to the reports of the events instead.

THE NEED FOR NUMERACY

Three broad groupings of activities in the practice of management are discernible. These are:

1 the execution of plans agreed upon, whose later amendment does not lie within the authority of those responsible for implementing them;
2 tactical decision-making;
3 strategic decision-making.

The distinction, for present purposes, between tactical and strategic decision-making is as follows. The tactical decision-maker is concerned with situations in which either all the factors are under his complete control, or else the factors which are outside his control are fixed and cannot be affected by his decision. The strategic decision-maker is concerned, on the other hand, with situations in which the factors which influence it are under the control of more than one operative, and where changes in the situation have repercussions outside the immediate area of activity to which the decision is applied.

A machine breakdown during production, which is capable of being put right in time to fulfil the production schedule laid down, and where all the facilities required to put it right under the control of the head of the department, requires a tactical decision on his part as to what should be done. A machine breakdown, which, it is clear, is going to result in the production schedule not being fulfilled as laid down, has repercussions in a number of directions, and requires an approach which is broader and can lead to the correct assessment of the results of alternative courses of action. Similarly, a branch bank manager with authority to grant loans up to a certain amount makes a tactical decision as to whether a particular application satisfies the conditions as laid down by policy, but recognizes that a loan of a larger amount necessitates a strategic decision involving the elements of the policy itself.

By definition, strategic decision-making requires a comprehensive approach, the identification and measurement of all the elements in a situation and an examination of their interrelationship. The evolution of activity from small-scale to large-scale produces as a natural consequence an increase in the number of decisions which are strategic rather than tactical. There occur, too, occasions when it is recognized that tactical decisions, which have hitherto been accepted as reasonably good approximations, are no longer good enough. The attribute which enables managers to make strategic decisions has been defined as numeracy. The need for numeracy has arisen partly as a consequence of natural evolution, but more explosively as a consequence of the second industrial revolution.

THE SECOND INDUSTRIAL REVOLUTION

The nineteenth century was one of magnificent achievement for industrial Britain. Once the revolution had been assimilated and the changes in organization and management practice had been accepted, Great Britain became the leader and pace-maker in the industrial world. Innovations, inventions and improvements in every aspect of industrial activity came thick and fast, but these were again of an evolutionary rather than a revolutionary character. Such was the case for about a century and a half. Then in the middle of the twentieth century came new developments to which the name revolution can legitimately be applied. Sometimes called the electronic revolution, perhaps more properly it should be called the second industrial revolution. To draw attention solely to the electronic aspects is to take too narrow a view by excluding those aspects relating to decision-making. Its course has remarkable similarities to the one followed by the first or mechanical revolution and the same characteristics can be discerned. Moreover, like the first, it was no sudden occurrence, but a movement spread over a period of time.

As with the first, it is difficult to define what the period is. The year 1966 is certainly too early a date to mark the culmination of the second revolution. Its start can perhaps, in round terms, be put at

1940, when it came to be realized by Turing of the National Physical Laboratory in London, and others, that the electronic techniques which were the basis of radar could be used to do mathematical calculations. Its duration is therefore at least twenty-seven years. This compares so far with a duration for the earlier revolution put at seventy years. Two factors may produce a shorter period for the present revolution. One is the very much more rapid pace of life in the twentieth century compared with the eighteenth. The other is that knowledge of the course of events of the first revolution may prevent protracted delays in taking each successive necessary step in the second. The characteristics of the first revolution, with some differences, find their parallel in the second.

SIMILARITIES BETWEEN THE FIRST AND SECOND INDUSTRIAL REVOLUTIONS

The concepts underlying the modern developments in equipment can be traced back to philosophers and mathematicians such as Pascal and Leibniz working in the latter half of the seventeenth century. Accompanying this new equipment are developments also in techniques of decision-making, which owe their origin to mathematicians of the seventeenth and eighteenth centuries who developed the theory of probability inspired by the activities of the gamblers with dice and at cards.

There were earlier developments both in equipment and in thinking which heralded the inventions and new ideas which were to come later. Pascal, for instance, built crude machines to perform adding and subtraction, and Leibniz constructed a similar type of machine to perform multiplication by successive addition. The most far-seeing of the earlier inventors in this field was, however, Charles Babbage, who was born in 1792 and lived to the age of eighty. He correctly deduced the logical principles of designing equipment to perform the operations of addition, subtraction, multiplication and division from which all forms of computation are built up. These principles he embodied in his 'analytical engine' and anticipated the methods of operation to be performed a century later in the computers of the electronic age. The required sequence of steps was to be communicated to his engine by a set of punched cards. These were not the punched cards of today, but cards used to control the Jacquard loom then being introduced into the cotton industry, and a strikingly early example of a numerate approach to controlling activity. Babbage correctly foresaw that, with a suitable code of orders to which the machine would react, the calculation and printing out of the numerical values of any given algebraic formula could easily be achieved. One of those who assisted Babbage in the preparation of the order sequences was Lord Byron's daughter, Lady Lovelace. The programmes, however, were never used operationally because the development of the machine was abandoned. Some parts of his machine are on view in the Science Museum, London, and Babbage has an honoured place in the history of the modern computer.

The symbol of the second industrial revolution is undoubtedly the electronic computer. It is as yet too early to say which of the stories surrounding the emergence of the electronic computer will become the equivalent of Watt and his mother's kettle. One which will have strong claims is the story of the food firm which became a computer manufacturer. The firm was J. Lyons and Co. Ltd. best known for their chain of tea shops. Always on the look-out for progressive ideas in the field of management accounting and office techniques, their organization and methods specialists were early attracted to the new developments in electronics. A team from the company visited the United States in 1947, and on their return were able to arrange for support to be given to the Cambridge University mathematical laboratory who were developing the Edsac, one of the first British computers. Convinced that a Lyons Electronic Office (as it came to be called) was not only a desirable thing to set up, but also a practical possibility, they sought the assistance of the office machine manufacturers in constructing it. But at that time in 1948 the office machine manufacturers were not interested in computers, and Lyons formed their own team to build a machine based on the ideas incorporated in the Cambridge Edsac. It was successful virtually from the beginning and became operational in 1951. Not only did it undertake the clerical work involved in supplying tea shops, calculate the payrolls and do other tasks for Lyons themselves, but it attracted such considerable attention in the commercial and industrial world that the firm found itself inundated with requests to show off the machine. So Leo Computers Ltd. was established to do computing work for Lyons, demonstrate the machine to others, undertake computing work on a service basis and ultimately build further machines for sale. This food firm proved to be not only one of the earliest, but also one of the most successful, computer manufacturing firms. This, however, is to do less than justice to the work of such pioneers as Wilkes, Wheeler and Gill at Cambridge, of Williams and Kilburn at Manchester, and of Wilkinson and Turing at the National Physical Laboratory. Nor would it be fair to minimize the contributions made by the firms of Ferranti Limited, English Electric Limited and Elliott Brothers Limited in the development and manufacture of the earliest computers.

The revolution really came to life when, as in the first form, the new form of power was linked to a new method of doing things. When electrical power was used in the form of electronics it could also measure information, store information and deduce from it. This provided the new concept for decision-making which justifies the description of revolution.

The new concepts received slow acceptance. Computers were certainly regarded as magnificent technical achievements, but for the scientists only. No office machine company could be found to build a computer for J. Lyons and Co. Ltd., and for a number of years manufacturers of punched card processing equipment did not allow their developments in electronics to stray far from a punched card base. On the side of the user, with the notable exception of J. Lyons and Co. Ltd., there were relatively few firms to be found prepared to try their hand at using computers for other than scientific work.

To get the most value from the new developments and new concepts, required a radical change in outlook towards the processing of data. Amongst those who accepted the need for change, the phrase 'integrated data processing' became current. This necessitates a departure from the old style of departments handling sections of work simultaneously but independently. Since many of them use the same initial data for their respective activities, this causes duplication of records of information, and produces final results from various departments which, to achieve accuracy, have to be reconciled with each other. Integrated data processing, by contrast, takes in the initial information once and for all, processes it centrally and in one operation makes the various calculations and deductions required. Reconciliation is performed as the operation proceeds. Underlying the change in outlook is the realization that the various sectional activities were never anything but parts of one comprehensive operation which, if it be economically possible, is better performed as a whole.

The development of the new equipment initially, as in the previous revolution, came from outside industry. The first steps were taken in academic circles in Cambridge and Manchester, and in the research laboratories of government establishments. The wealthy patrons of two centuries earlier were replaced by the support of government agencies such as the National Research Development Corporation, working through the newer science-based industries rather than the conventional business equipment firms. In the USA it was direct support from the departments of the Government which provided patronage on a wider scale than in Britain, and which by contrast was directed towards firms already concerned with developing business equipment.

Those parts of the new developments which did get taken up were, in the majority of cases, those which did not alter the existing way of doing things—Hargreaves' spinning jenny, so to speak, rather than Arkwright's water frame. Sometimes this would be by moving into improved versions of conventional equipment, some-times by extending mechanical punched card equipment to include electro-mechanical equipment or electronic calculators, sometimes by installing small-size electronic computers too small to achieve much, and sometimes by installing electronic computers of adequate capacity but using them to do the same things in the same way as before. Whatever the reasons that can be advanced to justify any of the courses of action listed, they all represent a holding back from taking advantage of the benefits of the new revolution.

THE DIFFERENCE BETWEEN THE REVOLUTIONS

Whether or not general acceptance of the new ideas will result in a general surge forward in the development of industrial and com-mercial Britain is a question for the future. Much leeway has to be made up to gain a leading position. Professor Stanley Gill of Imperial College, speaking at a symposium during the Business Efficiency Exhibition in London in 1963, painted a gloomy picture of the contrast between British and American attitudes to the second industrial revolution. He had this to say:

'I think that very few of us here have more than a dim under-standing of the kind of developments that are taking place today, of the things that we shall have to adopt in a very few years, many of which are already happening in other countries. The blame for this cannot be placed fully on any one section of the community; the cause lies in the heart of almost every British politician and business man. I began my career in scientific computing, but I have had some experience of lecturing and also trying to sell computers to business men both here and in the United States. Inevitably to start with, we only had experience of scientific computing. That was where the computers were first invented and scientific applications were very much easier to programme, so that is where we got started.

'To begin with, when we started with businessmen, the British businessman usually said, "Oh, come back and see me again when you have learned to speak my language". The American business-man usually said, "Please teach me your language so that I can understand what you are trying to say". In 1954, I took part in a course that was given at Massachusetts Institute of Technology by people who purely had experience in scientific computing, but it was advertised for business people, and quite a large number of businessmen came from all over the country. One of them from the East Coast was so impressed by this that, although his firm had no particular connection with electronics and was just an ordinary business firm, he felt that they should learn about this as quickly as possible. He invited me to go and spend a whole week delivering a series of lectures to some of the senior staff of the company. It was not an enormous company—I suppose the office staff didn't exceed one thousand or so—and yet they scraped up something like seventy or eighty people to come and hear about computers from myself, who had no experience of business at all. I just had to do my best to put computers in the businessman's language, and they were prepared to give up the time of seventy or eighty of their people for five lectures in that week on computers, and to hope that they would be able to extract enough from what I said to help them to understand this new business of computers. It seemed almost impossible to imagine anything of that kind happening in Britain. This was back in 1954, remember, when business applica-tions were practically unknown.'

By 1954, however, the Leo computer had been doing commercial work in Britain for three years. Even so, by 1963, when the words quoted above were spoken, little advance had been made. Part of the explanation for this was the high wage society in America which made it relatively more expensive to use computers in Britain than in America, and to this extent the positions of Britain and the United States had been reversed between the two revolutions. Exceptions could be made for the oil companies and one or two large organizations, but the general run of commercial and industrial firms were only just beginning to take action instead of watching from the sidelines. By 1966 signs were to be seen of an acceleration, but Britain, having once been in the forefront of the new revolution, was now well behind. The slow progress in the use of new equipment was paralleled by an equally slow progress in the understanding of the new thinking in decision-making which was being deployed in the fields of operational research. The work of leaders such as Stafford Beer and Professor Patrick Rivett went largely unfollowed except by those who were also pacemakers in the use of computers. Again, however, by 1966 there were signs that the dam was breaking and the business appointments columns of the newspapers were becoming filled with advertisements calling for candidates to be qualified in mathematics or to have experience in operational research.

THE IMPLICATIONS FOR MANAGEMENT

The changes now in progress as a result of developments in equipment and decision-making require changes in the practice of management. For Britain, the old comfortable dominating position meant that she could call the tune. The pace of business life was leisurely, competition was no great worry and prices could be fixed to permit the inclusion of large safety margins. The manager, alert as he was in recognizing the facts of the simple situations in which he found himself, and intelligent and energetic enough to decide on actions which would avoid disaster, was under no pressure. Any one of a number of reasonably good decisions, with a large safety margin built into it, would suffice.

Today the position is different. In no country in the world, least of all in Britain, is competition absent. The pace of business life is much greater and often such that little time is available for decision-making. Moreover, the factors involved in the situations facing the manager are both more numerous and more complex. With a much more difficult task to tackle he knows too that a large safety margin can no longer be built into his price. It is no longer sufficient to choose one of a number of reasonably good decisions. The decision must be the best possible one for his needs. The old attributes of strength of character, alertness and intelligence, together with the literacy which became necessary as a result of the first industrial revolution, though still required, are no longer sufficient. In order to understand the interplay of the forces affecting situations, to be able to measure their strengths and to deduce the consequences from their interplay and their strengths, the modern decision-maker requires the new attribute of numeracy.

The present revolution is still in progress, and how long it will take for its effects to be absorbed cannot be foretold. It is clear, however, that the appearance of commerce and industry and their pattern is altering. It would surely be surprising if the practice of management and the attributes of a manager were to remain un-altered as industry itself alters. Today it would be inconceivable to find an illiterate manager, and yet the period during which literacy has been a necessary attribute for a manager is very short compared with the time-span of organized man.

In the *Directory of National Biography* appear successive entries, two under the name of Crawshay. The Crawshays were the great iron-masters of South Wales and the entries are for the father, William (1788–1867) and his son, Robert (1817–79). Part of the entry for the elder reads, 'He was of all the Crawshays the finest type of the iron king. His will was law; in his home and business he tolerated no opposition. With his workmen he was strictly just. His quickness of perception and unhesitating readiness of decision and action make his success . . . .' There is much else besides, but of education there is no mention. If he had any, it was not considered relevant, for he preceded, in his working life, the effects of the first industrial revolution. The attributes he needed were strength of character, alertness and intelligence, and these he possessed in full measure. By contrast, almost the first item in the entry for the son is that he was educated at Dr Prichard's school at Llandaff.

Later entries refer to the education which it is now automatically assumed provides the literacy that had become a necessary attribute of the manager. No entry as yet draws attention specifically to any preparation that may have provided the attribute of numeracy. To read about this it will be necessary to wait for the entries for the next generation. Literacy was first acquired by the sons of the captains of industry of old, for it was they who were generally the successors of their fathers. It seems likely that in the same way numeracy will first be acquired by those who will succeed the present occupants of managing directors' chairs.

Being a numerate manager is not synonymous with being a mathematician any more than literacy implies an ability to write prize winning novels. Literacy consists of an awareness of the power of written words to describe events and the influences affecting events. It also consists of a knowledge of the grammar of using words in such a way that the meaning of the descriptions can be understood and communicated. Numeracy similarly consists of an awareness of the power of expressions, (which may sometimes be words and sometimes symbols), to describe the relationship of events and the strengths of the influences affecting them. It also consists of a knowledge of the grammar of using these expressions in such a way that the meaning of the relationships and the deductions from the strengths of the forces at work can be made correctly.

Numeracy is not the same as scientific management nor accounting, whether financial, cost or management accounting. Scientific management, as developed by F. W. Taylor and his successors, certainly shares some tools with numeracy, but uses them more narrowly to a particular area of the management problem which has been isolated for investigation. Numeracy operates on a broad front and never isolates any area, but always considers it in relation to all other relevant areas which it is its concern to identify and measure. Accounting, too, shares some of the tools of measurement with numeracy, but is concerned with facts that are known with certainty, either because they are historical or because they are elements in possible courses of action which have already been defined. Numeracy, however, operates more widely and concerns itself not only with certainty but with uncertainty and the assessment of relationships between uncertain events, while it never starts by defining in advance any course of action. It is concerned to deduce by logical thought processes from the complete range of possible courses what the right course is for any particular purpose.

To become a numerate manager may seem a formidable task, but the formidable tasks of one era are the commonplaces of the next. The parts of this task can be identified as:

1 knowing those techniques of numerate decision-making which exist and of their uses;
2 assessing the perspective of numeracy in relation to other aspects of management;
3 understanding the characteristics of information and data processing;
4 forming opinions on the implication of numeracy for the development of managers.

These will be examined in the following chapters.

CHAPTER II

SOME TOOLS OF NUMERACY

THE numerate manager will wish to avail himself of whatever aids seem likely to prove useful. These aids may consist either of equipment which will help him in the physical aspects of his decision-making, or of techniques which will assist him in the conceptual aspects. This chapter will deal with some of the techniques that have been used successfully in recent years. These techniques have been grouped together as a body of knowledge to which the name operational research has been given.

The industrial development of all nations has been punctuated roughly every quarter of a century with wars. The wars of the most recent century have been on such a scale that normal progress in industry became impossible as production facilities were switched over to a war footing. There were compensations in the long run. The unstinted allocation of resources in certain directions far in excess of anything seen in peace-time and the powerful incentive given by the need to survive provide conditions in which research, both physical and intellectual, have the most favourable opportunities of success. Many of the results, used in the meantime to prosecute the wars, are found when fighting ceases to be applicable to peace-time industrial affairs.

From the war of 1939–45 two developments, one physical and one intellectual, were of special interest to industry. The first, radar, has already been mentioned. The invention of radar and the knowledge which came from the use of pulse techniques in the detection of enemy aircraft, and from applying electronics generally to the control of equipment, led directly to the invention of electronic computers and of equipment for industrial process control. The second came out of the processes employed in war-time decision-making.

The scale and scope of warfare had grown to such an extent by the outbreak of the First World War in 1914 that it could no longer be fought by compact professional armies augmented where necessary by volunteers. The introduction of conscription became inevitable. The same situation arose in the Second World War to an even greater extent. The result was that before very long there were not only in subordinate positions, but in positions of command, men who had until a short time previously been engaged in their civilian occupations and had no real knowledge, and certainly no experience, of waging war. Many such found themselves taking part in the planning and direction of operations. At the same time the progress that had been made and continued to be made in science and technology was at such a pace that the equipment with which wars had earlier been fought, and the methods of fighting, rapidly became out of date. The equipment was superseded by new strange devices. Nobody really knew what were the right methods of fighting wars in these new conditions.

The problems, new, larger in scale than ever before and much more complex though they were, had nevertheless to be solved. The methods of solving them which ultimately proved successful were numerate methods, and the techniques used were those which came to be known as operational research techniques. The method essentially consisted of forming operational research teams made up of men and women with varying backgrounds, but each distinguished in possessing some special knowledge and with ability to apply it. The teams had no option but to tackle their problems from basic first principles and proceed to a solution by logical deduction, measuring with the greatest accuracy possible all the relevant factors.

There is an example from the Atlantic sector of the war which is a classic in the history of operational research and illustrates numeracy in action.

The problem was the lack of success of aircraft on anti-submarine patrol in the Atlantic in their efforts to destroy submarines by dropping depth charges on them. The circumstances, as stated, were that it could be assumed that the submarines would not be surprised by the aircraft and would have time to dive. The fuse fitted to the depth charge would allow the charges to be exploded at depths of 35 feet or more. The pilot had no time to set the fuse before making his attack. Therefore all fuses were pre-set and the depth chosen was 100 feet. The question put was this. Of all the possible depths at which the fuse could be set, i.e. all depths of 35 feet or more, was 100 feet the correct one?

Numeracy requires that the problem should be considered in fundamental terms. It can be rephrased as follows. There are two moving bodies, a submarine and a depth charge. The submarine can move vertically, horizontally and in any direction of the compass. The depth charge is projected in a fixed direction for a given time. Damage will be caused to the submarine if it is within a certain radius of the depth charge when the latter goes off. What is the probability of the submarine being within a sphere of given radius of the depth charge at the end of the time given for it to go off? The moment when this will occur is given by the time the depth charge will take to reach a depth of 100 feet along the path on which it is travelling, so the position of the depth charge is known exactly. The question is where the first body will be at that time. When it is remembered that the submarine can move in any direction, it will easily be seen that its position at any particular time can never be known exactly. However, the *probability* of its being within a sphere of a particular radius from the depth charge can be calculated. When this was done, it was found that this probability was very low indeed, so it was not surprising that the results were poor. Further calculations showed that for all depths of 35 feet or more the probabilities were always low.

Numeracy, however, also requires that the problem should be considered in the broadest possible way, and so this particular problem should also be examined without the restriction that the point of meeting is at a depth of 35 feet or more. Now, although the submarine can always move in any direction, the earlier it can be caught the smaller will be the space needed to cover all the possible positions it can reach after the allowed time has elapsed. So the probability of its being within a sphere of a given radius centred on points at a depth of less than 35 feet is greater than if centred on points at a depth of 35 feet or more.

There is one other factor, however. What is the probability of the submarine having travelled less than 35 feet vertically, as against the probability of its having travelled 35 feet or more vertically? To get some idea of this it is necessary to go back to the original framework of the problem. The answer depends on how quickly the submarine gets moving.

The final answer came from combining these two factors, and it turned out to be that the fuses should be set so that the charges exploded at a depth of 25 feet. This caused some trouble, because so sure had the planners been that the submarines would dive at least 35 feet that the fuses had been designed in such a way that it was impossible for the charges to explode at less than 35 feet.

However, a numerate manager has the courage to act on a logical conclusion and the fuses were redesigned.

The results were startling and the number of successes immediately shot up. It has been reported that captured German submarine commanders, after the change, expressed the belief that the increased sinkings were due to an increase in the explosive power of the depth charges. The results were achieved at only the cost of redesigning the fuse.

This problem required for its solution a knowledge of probability theory and some not-too-complicated calculations. Numeracy accepts that on occasions some quite complicated mathematics may be necessary. This can make the technique itself rather difficult to understand. A more fruitful approach is to consider the types of problem for whose solution various techniques have been developed. These can be grouped as follows:

> Problems of identification
> Problems of conflict
> Problems of unrestrained allocation
> Problems of restrained allocation
> Waiting time problems
> Problems of strategy.

Each of these categories will be considered in turn.

PROBLEMS OF IDENTIFICATION

The simplest type of problem occurs when it is known that a factor in the situation being examined possesses a characteristic which is important but whose exact nature has not yet been revealed. The problem is to identify it from whatever facts are available. Frequently the characteristic that it is sought to identify will be a numerical value.

Consider the commonplace situation of ordering supplies of material to meet a production schedule when there are no questions to decide as to who the supplier shall be and no problems arise as to price and delivery. In such a situation the only problem is to decide how much to order. If the amount already in stock is known and the total amount required to meet the schedule is known, then few people would experience any difficulty in finding the amount that should be ordered. To take an example: 350 pounds of the material is in stock, 500 pounds is needed to meet the schedule, so

150 pounds needs to be ordered. The act of subtracting the 350 from the 500 is so much second nature, done without consciously thinking about it, that the analysis of the problem is masked. The analysis goes as follows: the known amount of the material that is in stock added to the unknown amount that must be ordered must equal the known amount that is needed for the production schedule:

$$(amount\ in\ stock) + (amount\ to\ be\ ordered)$$
$$= (amount\ needed\ for\ schedule).$$

This statement is an equation.

The task that is set is to discover the amount to be ordered. This can be achieved if another equation can be formed in which the left-hand side consists only of what has to be discovered and the right-hand side consists of things that are known.

This second equation must be formed by logical deduction from the first equation, which is all there is to go on. To help with the logic there are certain self-evident truths or axioms that can be used. One of these is that if the same amount is taken away from equal quantities then the remainders are equal. This leads directly to the following result:

$$(amount\ to\ be\ ordered) = (amount\ needed\ for\ schedule)$$
$$-(amount\ in\ stock).$$

This equation states the general rule to be followed for obtaining the amount to be ordered. The operation is now performed merely as an act of arithmetic but its justification rests on the steps of logical analysis by which it was first derived and of which the arithmetic is the final step in a particular case.

When the argument and analysis are stated in plain language, as has been done, the lack of succinctness is apparent. Contrast this with the same argument expressed in mathematical language.

Let x be the amount to be ordered

a be the amount in stock

b be the amount needed for the schedule.

Then

$$a+x = b$$

therefore

$$x = b-a$$

D

In this particular case

$$b = 500$$

$$a = 350$$

therefore

$$x = 150.$$

That is, the amount to be ordered is 150, as before.

Consider another example. In this case the production load in a factory in the appropriate units for the product is made up partly of a fixed contract and partly by the orders the sales force get in. Let us suppose each salesman obtains orders for three units per month and the fixed contract brings in ten units per month. Then if P stands for the production load per month and x is the number of men in the sales force, the statement of the situation can be written in mathematical language as:

$$P = 10 + 3x$$

This statement can now be used either to calculate the production load per month if the number of salesmen is known, or to calculate how many salesmen are needed to give any particular production load for the factory. Suppose, for instance, that the full capacity of the factory per month is 100 units, then the equation provides the means of calculating the number of salesmen required. It can now be written:

$$100 = 10 + 3x$$

or

$$3x + 10 = 100$$

which is saying the same thing. Then, by similar rules of mathematical grammar to those used in the previous example,

$$3x = 100 - 10$$

$$= 90$$

and so

$$x = 30$$

So 30 salesmen are needed to fill the factory.

This example can be extended to cover the case where the salesmen are of two kinds, senior salesmen and trainee salesmen. To preserve the balance of the sales force, it may be laid down as a matter of policy that there must always be 10 more senior salesmen than there are trainee salesmen. This policy condition can be written in mathematical language as $x - y = 10$, if x represents the senior salesmen and y represents the trainee salesmen.

If each senior salesman is capable of taking orders for 3 units per month and each trainee salesman is capable of taking 2 orders per month, and it is also laid down that the factory, which is capable of turning out 100 units per month, must be kept up to full capacity, then this statement can be written as

$$3x + 2y + 10 = 100$$

So we have

$$3x + 2y = 90$$
$$x - y = 10$$

This is a pair of simultaneous equations and using the rules of mathematical grammar appropriate to solving simultaneous equations it can be found that $x = 22$ and $y = 12$. Clearly $x - y = 10$, and the total order is

$$(3 \times 22) + (2 \times 12) = 66 + 24 = 90$$

which together with the fixed contract of 10 keeps the factory up to full capacity. So there must be 22 senior salesmen and 12 trainee salesmen.

Problems of identification can always be solved by translating the statements of policy and the characteristics of the situation into the language of mathematics and then using the appropriate rules of mathematical grammar to find the solution.

The numerate manager is not himself required to apply the rules. In the examples cited he might well be able to do so, but in other cases the appropriate rules might demand a deeper knowledge of mathematics and specialist services would be called upon. The numerate manager does, however, appreciate that this class of problem is capable of being solved neatly by translating it into mathematical language. He ought, too, to be able to discuss it with his specialist, since it is his duty to make the statements which are to be translated. He will find it of advantage therefore to be aware of some of the tricks of translation.

Of the three examples cited, for instance, the first was based on the single entity of the quantity of material to be ordered and expressible by the variable x. The second was based on a step-by-step relationship between the sales and the number of salesmen. This was expressed by multiplying the variable symbol for the number of salesmen by a constant as a coefficient. The coefficient would be a symbolic letter in a general case, and in a particular case would be a number. The third example illustrates the same step-by-step or linear relationship, but introduces a second letter y, because there are now two unknown variables. The usual symbols for variables are x, y and z, and these can be extended by adding suffixes to indicate further items in the same class. Thus:

$$x_1 \; x_2 \; x_3 \; x_4 \text{ etc.}$$
$$y_1 \; y_2 \; y_3 \; y_4 \text{ etc.}$$
$$z_1 \; z_2 \; z_3 \; z_4 \text{ etc.}$$

can be used for several items in class x, several items in class y and several items in class z.

Other relationships and the mode of expressing them are:

1 The squared relationships, when a doubling of the initial measurement results in four times the value accruing. This is expressed by using x^2 as a variable.

2 The cube relationship, when a doubling of the initial measurement results in eight times the value accruing. This is expressed by using x^3 as a variable.

3 In general the power relationship, when a doubling of the initial measurement results in 2^n times the value accruing. This is expressed by using x^n as a variable.

4 When the rate of increase of the value is directly proportional to the value itself and hence increasing by bigger and bigger steps, it is said to be increasing exponentially and the variable is expressed by e^x.

5 Decreases in value can be expressed by using the reciprocal, namely $1/x$, or $1/x^2$, or $1/x^3$, or in general $1/x^n$.

6 When the value is decreasing by bigger and bigger steps, it is said to be decreasing exponentially, and the variable is expressed by e^{-x}.

The first three examples and the six further ones listed are the commonest types of relationships found. More detailed explanations of some of the terms used will be found in the vocabulary contained in the glossary at the end of this book.

PROBLEMS OF CONFLICT

The possibility of stating business problems in simple algebraic equation form, and of using elementary methods of solving them, occurs most frequently when all the factors in the situation are exerting the same sort of influence and are all pointing in the same direction.

However, this is rarely the situation in business. Some of the factors in a given situation pull in one direction, others push in the opposite direction, yet others in a third and a fourth direction, and so on. The problem that exists is to find the best method of combining these conflicting factors so as to give the best result for the business as a whole. This is often called seeking a compromise, but this is quite the wrong word, for compromise today has a connotation of something less than the best.

It is not something less than the best which is being sought. It is the *best* solution that is wanted, but the best solution for the business as a whole and not for any one section of it.

Problems of conflict occur in any part of a business. They are probably the biggest single class of business problem. In fixing the length of a production run, for instance, the production factors all point to as long a run as possible. There will be less down time from changing machines, fewer teething troubles as machines start up, greater productivity as operators get used to the set-up and so on. The sales division, on the other hand, do not take kindly to selling nothing but one variety one year and nothing but another variety the next. They want a judicious mixture of varieties to sell in quantities which will just keep pace with their selling efforts. The warehouse too will have views which may be different from either the production department or the sales division. To get the right length of production run involves solving a problem of conflict.

Or consider the work of a purchasing department. Costs of operation would be very low if on the first day of the year one single purchasing requisition could be prepared for the whole of the materials required for that year. It takes very little extra time to type 12,000 tons rather than 1,000 tons, but to type another eleven requisitions on the first day of each following month requires the details of supplier, unit, price, addresses and so on to be typed twelve times instead of once. Purchasing departments would like to order the materials in as large quantities as possible. The storage department, on the other hand, face considerable difficulties in handling quantities larger than their space, work force and equipment is geared to receive. There are other factors involved, such as discounts for bulk purchase, phased deliveries and the cost of tying up capital in stocks. Again, it is a problem of conflict, and the same problem as that of fixing the right length of production run.

This is also the case in the personnel field, when a situation arises where the work to be done is more than can be performed by the work force in a normal working day. One solution would be to work overtime, and this would entail certain costs arising from the payment of overtime rates. An alternative solution would be to engage new staff. The overtime costs would be saved, but instead there would be costs of advertising, costs of engagement and costs of training. Again it is a problem of conflict.

Numeracy requires that these should be recognized as one and the same problem and not as separate production problems, purchasing organization problems and personnel problems. When this is done it is discovered that it is a type of problem in which mathematicians have been interested for a very long time, and for which the differential calculus was used in order to provide methods of finding solutions. Defined in fundamental terms, it consists of combining together certain elements, each of which varies in different degrees, in such a way that an optimum result is obtained. The answer obtained will not be the best answer for the production department or the sales division or the warehouse, for example, but it will provide the greatest measure of the defined efficiency for the business as a whole.

A solution could be found through examining a range of possibilities chosen by varying judiciously all the different factors and evaluating the results for selected values. This would be tedious and open to the objection that, since only some of the possibilities can be evaluated, there is no guarantee that the real solution has not been missed. Moreover, tables of figures are not the easiest things to display in readable form, and even if the correct solution is identified the force of its impact may be weakened in this form of presentation.

A better method of presentation is to show the situation graphically. Consider the problem of choosing the length of production run which will make the costs as low as possible. The cost per unit of output for varying lengths of production run can be worked out by standard costing methods. Confining attention to lengths of production run which are possible without increasing the capital invested, the situation to be represented will be one of cost decreasing as the production run increases in length and will be of the form shown graphically in Figure 3.

At the same time, however, the opposite is happening for the sales division. More of one product than can be sold by normal

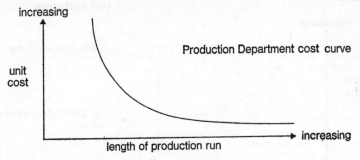

FIG. 3.—Production department cost curve.

methods becomes an embarrassment and results in a unit cost which increases as the production run increases in length. The situation for the sales division will be of the form shown graphically in Figure 4.

Neither of these two sections of the business can, however, be allowed to dictate the solution. A managerial decision at higher level is required to resolve the conflict, and the basis for the decision will be the behaviour of the total unit costs, combining both production and sales factors. This will be of the form shown in Figure 5, where the dotted curve represents the combined cost curve.

Point A is the point on the total cost curve where the unit cost is lowest. This is the point in which the manager is interested. The length of production run which gives this lowest cost is given by dropping a perpendicular line from A to the length of production run line. In Figure 5, Point B is the point representing the length of

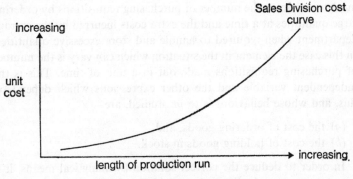

FIG. 4.—Sales division cost curve.

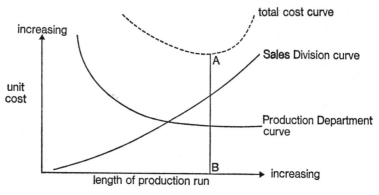

FIG. 5.—Combined production and sales cost curve.

production run which gives the lowest total unit cost. If it is not convenient, or if it is thought to be tedious, to draw the graphs, then this type of problem can be solved in a third way. This is to solve it by analysis, using the techniques of the differential calculus. These the mathematician has developed to help him to discover maximum or minimum solutions. The analysis is in two parts, of which the second consists of following automatically a set of logical rules. The first part, which from a management point of view is the more important, comprises the identification of the elements of the problem and their expression in mathematical terms. The problem, being a fundamental one, can be put into a variety of frameworks. The graphical solution was described in terms of length of production run. The analytical solution will be described in terms of purchasing policy.

The conflict here lies between the desire of the purchasing department to cut down the number of purchasing requisitions by ordering large quantities at a time and the extra costs incurred by the storage department when required to handle and store excessive quantities. In this case the element in the situation which can vary is the number of purchasing requisitions made out in a unit of time. This is the independent variable and the other expressions which depend on this, and whose behaviour is to be studied, are

(*a*) the cost of ordering goods, and
(*b*) the cost of holding goods in stock.

In order to deduce the correct solution by analytical means, it is necessary first to identify and measure the elements in the situation.

The situation will be taken to be that of a seasonal product in which the stock of raw materials is reduced to zero at the end of the period. The elements then are:

1 The total requirements for the period in question; this is designated as D.
2 The number of requisitions made out in the period; this is designated as n, and the problem consists of finding the economic value for n.
3 The quantity to be specified on the requisition as the ordering quantity; this is designated as ϕ and if, for simplicity, it is assumed that the materials are used at a steady rate, then this quantity will be constant, and when multiplied by the number or requisitions must be equal to the total requirements. So

$$\phi = D/n.$$

4 A measure of the cost of preparing one purchasing requisition; this is designated as P.
5 A measure of the cost of holding in stock one unit; this is designated as S.
6 The average amount in stock during the unit of time. This can be derived by taking the average of the amount in stock at the beginning of the time span, just after a delivery has been made, and the amount in stock at the end of the time span. The amount in stock at the beginning of the time span is ϕ and the amount in stock at the end is zero. So the average is $\phi/2$ or $D/2n$.

From these elements we can build up in mathematical form a statement of what the total cost will be. This is made up of two parts: the cost of preparing orders and the cost of holding a stock. Thus

$$\text{total cost} = Pn + \frac{SD}{2n}$$

This is the first part of the analysis complete. The second part consists of applying the techniques of the differential calculus in order to find out when this total cost will be a minimum. When this is done, it will be found that

$$n = \sqrt{\frac{S \times D}{2P}}$$

From this it can be calculated that the quantity which should be ordered on each requisition should be

$$\sqrt{\frac{2PD}{S}}$$

Mathematically, the answers obtained may involve a fraction and would then, in practice, be rounded off. Equally, account would have to be taken of the standard packs in which the supplier provided the material to be ordered and the value thrown up by the calculation adjusted suitably.

Before any analysis could begin, it was necessary to establish the pattern of the backcloth. In the example just considered it was assumed:

1 that the total requirements were spread uniformly over the period;

2 that the quantity required was known with certainty;

3 that it was possible to make the cost estimates;

4 that there were no other factors with an influence on the situation.

Given that this was the correct backcloth, then logical analysis established both the frequency with which requisitions should be prepared and the quantity which should be ordered on each occasion. One is tempted to react that in the circumstances of this example, if the frequency with which requisitions should be prepared is known, then a knowledge of what quantity should be ordered follows automatically. This is true. What is important is to realize that it is automatic because it follows from a step in the logical analysis which is accepted without questioning. In reality it is no more automatic than the earlier part of the analysis or any piece of mathematical analysis correctly applied. The numerate manager accepts this and concerns himself with ensuring that the correct piece of analysis is used, that it is correctly applied, and that the pattern to which it is applied is correctly identified and assessed. From then on, he knows that the deduction follows quite automatically. For the first of these tasks he will have his specialists to assist him in the field of decision-making, as in any other, but decision-making is his own province and total ignorance of the specialist knowledge in this field will lessen his effectiveness as a decision-maker. For the correct application of the analysis the manager's function is to choose either a human agent or a machine.

The manager's biggest responsibility is to establish the pattern of the backcloth. In the example considered, for instance, if the requirements are not spread uniformly over the period, the specification of how the requirements are spread must be on the authority of the manager. It is for the specialist then to translate this into his working language. At least two possibilities are open to him. He may, on the one hand, find a mathematical expression which satisfactorily represents the spread of requirements. On the other hand, he may shorten the unit of time to a period in which for all practical purposes the spread is uniform and then build up a changing purchasing policy from these shorter periods.

It is often objected that mathematical analysis is not a valid method of solution for want of certainty in the figures used. There are several weaknesses in this objection. The first is that there are many techniques available for dealing with figures which are not known with any certainty. The insurance companies operate entirely on probabilities and actuarial science has contributed much to the knowledge of these techniques. The second is that there never is, by *any* method, any certainty in business decision-making and the whole of business operations concerns itself with risk-taking. Mathematical analysis can be used to define the risk that has to be taken in following particular courses of action. The third weakness is that the result of the analysis is not an end in itself, but a basis for determining the course of action which is to be followed. In contrast to many areas in science the number of possible courses of action in business is relatively few. The same course of action is likely to follow from a wide range of results of the analysis. If then, while still unable to define the figures used with exactness, it is possible to state upper and lower limits beyond which the figures will not lie, the analysis can be performed twice, using the upper and lower figures in turn. If the same course of action would result in either case, then more often than not it is immaterial where exactly the real figure lies. Quite often this will be sufficient, because business decision-making is fortunately not sensitive to small changes in circumstance. It will happen, however, that sometimes the two calculations will produce two separate courses of action that should be followed. In those cases it is necessary either to try again to arrive at a narrower span for the limits, or to abandon any thought of using analysis and resort to more arbitrary methods of decision-making.

The objection may be raised that not all the factors in the situation have been taken into account. In the example considered only two factors were included. The method of analysis, however, is independent of the number of factors involved, and if all have not been specified the fault lies at the door of the manager. The responsibility for specifying them is his. It may be pleaded that the reason for not specifying them is that they cannot be measured. This may be so, but it does not necessarily matter. The purpose of the analysis is to establish a correct course of action, and for this purpose in very many instances only a knowledge of the *relative* values of the factors, one to another, is needed. The *absolute* values are not necessary for the analysis to proceed. Often when the absolute values cannot be determined the relative values can, and this will then suffice.

One of the major areas in which conflict occurs is inventory control. Here the conflict arises between the penalty that occurs in the shape of lost goodwill or lost orders from customers when one runs out of stock, and the disinclination to incur extra costs by maintaining unnecessarily high stocks. The analysis can be done to a much greater depth and to a greater degree of intricacy than has so far been described. The theory for doing this is known. This is only one of the areas where conflict exists. The problem is a fundamental one. Wherever conflict exists and the conditions for stating the problem can be specified and a criterion for judging the solution can be defined, then the methods described in this section can be used. These are big 'ifs' of course, and managers have the right and the duty to concern themselves with them. What is not rational is to reject the whole process as invalid on the grounds that, being sophisticated, it is somehow different in kind from the more familiar and well understood thought processes of simpler forms of decision-making described as problems of identification.

PROBLEMS OF UNRESTRAINED ALLOCATION

Problems of conflict, dealt with in the previous section, constitute the largest class of problem to be found in business. The second largest class probably comprises problems of allocation.

Again it is a fundamental and universal type of problem. It may be a question of machines to execute orders, and the measure of efficiency may be the length of time required to complete a whole batch of orders. Or it may be girls in an office faced with work which includes taking shorthand dictation and subsequent typing, audio-typing, copy-typing, working duplicating machines and filing. Each of the girls is able to do any of the jobs, but some are senior girls and some are junior girls. So there are different costs incurred according to which girl is used. This arises from two causes, on the one hand the salary that is paid to her and on the other how well she does each of the jobs. A cost can be established for using each of the girls on each of the jobs, and the problem consists of preparing a work schedule which will keep costs at their lowest.

Allocation problems arise frequently in planning the distribution of goods. The output of various factories sited in different parts of the country has to be allocated to depots sited also in different parts of the country. Electrical generating stations operate at maximum efficiency with coal of a particular thermal capacity appropriate to its design and with varying degrees of efficiency according to which particular type of coal is actually used. The various types of coal come from different collieries and the transport costs will differ according to distance and the available means of transport. An efficient purchasing policy must take all these factors into account in deciding which is the best pattern of allocating the coal needed.

The oil companies have a similar problem in deciding the operating schedules for their tanker distribution fleet. At any one moment of time, tankers are empty after discharging their loads in a series of ports throughout the world. In a second series of ports are new consignments of oil waiting to be picked up. Yet a third series of ports provides destinations for these new consignments. Large sums of money in the shape of savings in distribution costs are at stake in choosing the right pattern of allocating which empty tanker should go to which port to go to which further destination.

The preparation of schedules of production or allocation schedules in general is a business practice dating back a long way. The normal method employed is essentially one of trial and error—making a first shot at a schedule, assessing it, amending it and continuing to do so until by some criterion it can be considered satisfactory. Experience counts for a lot, and schedulers of long standing have at their command personally developed rules to guide them in their choice of amendments. The result may be considered good enough but, unless every single different pattern of allocation has been considered, they can never know for certain whether the pattern finally chosen is the *best possible*. Empirical rules for the choice of amendments can never indicate that a stage has been reached when no further improvement in the schedule is possible. If it is desirable to know what is the very best schedule possible, there is no help for it but to work out every one. In any but the simplest of situations this is a daunting task and usually, in the time available, impossible of fulfilment.

Consider, for example, a situation where any of three machines *A*, *B* and *C* can do any of three jobs *1*, *2* and *3*. There are these possible allocation patterns:

1	2	3
A does Job *1*	*A* does Job *2*	*A* does Job *3*
while *B* does Job *2*	while *B* does Job *1*	while *B* does Job *1*
and *C* does Job *3*	and *C* does Job *3*	and *C* does Job *2*

4	5	6
A does Job *1*	*A* does Job *2*	*A* does Job *3*
while *B* does Job *3*	while *B* does Job *3*	while *B* does Job *2*
and *C* does Job *2*	and *C* does Job *1*	and *C* does Job *1*

In this case there are six different patterns of allocation. This conclusion could be reached by another route. One of the machines has to be considered first. Let this be machine *A*. It can be allotted to any one of three jobs. That is, there are three ways of dealing with machine *A*. For *each* of the ways of allotting machine *A* there are *two* ways of allotting machine *B* to a job. So the number of ways of allotting *both* machines *A* and *B* is three multiplied by 2, i.e. 6.

Number of ways of allotting two machines $= 3 \times 2$.

There are 6 ways of dealing with machines *A* and *B*, but there is now only one job left. There is one machine, *C*, unallotted. It can only be allotted to the one job not on a machine and there is only one way of doing this. This is true for *each* of the 6 ways of allotting machines *A* and *B*. So the number of ways of allotting all 3 machines *A*, *B* and *C* is 6 multiplied by one, i.e. 6.

Number of ways of allotting three machines $= 3 \times 2 \times 1$.

This argument was developed by choosing the order of allotting the machines to be *A* then *B* then *C*. It would not have mattered, however, if the machines had been allotted in a different order. The argument would have been the same and so, as before, the number of different patterns of allocation in this case is six. It is more meaningful, however, to express the statement as follows:

The number of ways of allotting 3 machines to 3 jobs is

$$3 \times 2 \times 1.$$

By a similar argument it can be stated that the number of ways of allotting 4 machines to 4 jobs is

$$4 \times 3 \times 2 \times 1,$$

and, for a further example, the number of ways of allotting 10 machines to 10 jobs is

$$10 \times 9 \times 8 \times 7 \times 6 \times 5 \times 4 \times 3 \times 2 \times 1.$$

This can be generalized to state that the number of ways of allotting n machines to n jobs is

$$n \times (n-1) \times (n-2) \times (n-3) \times \ldots \times 4 \times 3 \times 2 \times 1.$$

n in any particular case takes its appropriate value. In the example given where there were 3 machines, n was 3. Where there are 8 machines and 8 jobs to do, n is 8, and so on.

With only 3 facilities and three needs, the task of inspecting all the 6 possible allocation patterns is not heavy. With 4 facilities and needs, the task of inspecting all the 24 possible allocation patterns is still tolerable. With 5 facilities and needs, the number of allocation patterns increases to 120, and with 6 to 720. The task of inspecting all allocation patterns soon becomes one that cannot be contemplated. Experience will provide some guiding rules as to which patterns can safely be excluded from inspection, and experience can help to select what may be good patterns, but experience cannot lay down universal rules for selection, nor can it indicate that the best pattern has been found and that no further inspection is necessary.

In the case of certain backcloths to this type of problem a technique is available which enables the best solution to an allocation problem to be identified with absolute certainty. This statement needs a minor qualification to the effect that there may be other patterns which are as good as the one identified. There will, however, be none which is better. The technique is known as linear programming. Where it can be used it is an exceedingly powerful technique, but the circumstances in which it can be applied need to be understood. These circumstances are that, where changes in whatever expression is being used to measure efficiency occur, they are in direct proportion to changes in the elements determining the efficiency. There is thus a fixed ratio between any particular element and its contribution to efficiency. The effect of changes in the quantity of materials used in a manufacturing process illustrate this. With a fixed price for the material, halving the quantity of material used will halve the contribution made by the material cost to the total cost. Doubling it would double its contribution. If the relationship were displayed graphically, the shape of the graph would be a straight line. It is this fact which gives its name to the technique—linear programming.

Linear programming is a method which also operates by successive trials. In this it does not differ from the methods used by any programme scheduler, experienced or otherwise. There are, however, some important differences which provide the technique with its power. The scheduler using his own methods of trial and error will sometimes succeed in finding a better solution than the best one so far found and sometimes he will not. Moreover, he will keep on trying the effect of this or that alteration blindly until he decides to call it a day. What the technique of linear programming succeeds in doing, on the other hand, is to provide a set of rules which will ensure that each successive trial produces at least as good and usually a better solution than the last one. Moreover, one of the rules provides a means of knowing whether or not any improvement is possible. So that ultimately there is a clear indication that it is not possible to progress any further to a better solution.

The advantages of using linear programming are two-fold. First, because rules are known to guide progress and time is not wasted in trying solutions which cannot lead to an improvement, and secondly because ultimately it is known that no further improvement is possible and the best solution is therefore known with certainty. In practice, it is likely that initially the improvements in successive trials may be large. As further improvements are made, the degree of the improvement becomes less and less. After a certain stage the amount of improvement that is being obtained by further trials is becoming less than is considered worthy of further expenditure of effort and the exercise is usually halted.

There are two main classes of allocation problem. The first of these arises where the number of facilities is the same as the number of needs. This is the type which has been illustrated and examples can normally be found in problems of job assignment. The second class occurs where the number of facilities is different from the number of needs and is usually given the name of transportation problem. In the assignment technique, it is assumed that the whole of any facility is assigned to one need. In the transportation technique, it is permitted to divide up a facility between a number of needs. Thus, for instance, a transportation problem may be set up to formulate a policy whereby the output from seven factories in different parts of the country could be distributed to fourteen depots located in yet other parts of the country at the lowest possible cost in transport.

The mathematician has at his command two different techniques, each appropriate to the class of problem, although it is possible to transform one class into the other with a little ingenuity. The name 'transportation' comes from the fact that the technique has been applied to problems of distribution. Sometimes this is in order to decide the right pattern, at other times, from a pattern which is taken as fixed, to decide on the correct location for the facility concerned. One fruitful area for applying this technique is in choosing the site for a new warehouse, resiting warehouses or discovering how to combine many warehouses into a few. The location of oil refineries and power stations has also been tackled in this way. The same technique has been applied to solve problems not connected with transport, as for instance in the blending of teas or in the formulation of a production facility to provide for the most efficient use of a group of catalytic crackers in an oil refinery, or to decide on the layout for the pipework in a factory in order to minimize construction costs.

Summarizing, allocation problems arise when a set of facilities is available to meet a set of needs. Each of the facilities is able to satisfy each of the needs but with varying degrees of efficiency. The measure by which efficiency is judged is defined. The problem is to discover which allocation pattern will produce the maximum efficiency according to the measure laid down. If the relationships are linear, then certain of the techniques of linear programming can be used to provide solutions.

PROBLEMS OF RESTRAINED ALLOCATION

In considering problems of unrestrained allocation, it was assumed that any solution which was found by the mathematical techniques could be applied in practice. This is naturally not always the case.

E

For instance, it might be found that the best site for a warehouse in strictly mathematical terms was, for example, in the middle of Lake Windermere. One would normally assume that this was not a valid solution; although in passing it should be stated that the reasons for discarding a solution must be equally valid. Impossibility should not be confused with difficulty and if, for example, the economic advantages of having a warehouse in the middle of Lake Windermere were overwhelming, it might well justify the costs involved in obtaining planning permission to do so, and in sinking piles or providing some other means of supporting the warehouse.

In the majority of cases of allocation restraints are in operation, and the following illustration is typical. A firm of cattle-food manufacturers is faced with a sudden emergency. The supply of many of the essential oils used in the manufacture is cut off. New recipes have to be devised and there are many ingredients that can be considered. However, even if the cow is prepared to eat anything that is set before it, the farmer has his own views as to what he is prepared to pay his money for. He requires that there should be at least a certain minimum quantity of protein in the pack, and not more than a certain maximum quantity of carbohydrate. He may, too, specify both a minimum and a maximum quantity of iodine, and so on with other ingredients. Any solution that is to be feasible must satisfy these restraints. This still leaves, of course, in most applications a very large number of possible recipes, and the manufacturer is concerned to find which of these he can produce at the lowest cost. This type of problem is in consequence often known as a 'least cost mix problem'.

The person who is going to use the solution is, of course, fully entitled to impose what restraints he wishes. He has, however, a duty to think out the problem in advance of a solution being worked out. What ought not to be open to him and, if he is numerate, would not be contemplated by him, is to wait until the solution to a problem as specified has been found and then to reject it as being impractical because of certain conditions which have now occurred to him. If the conditions have to be imposed because of new circumstances which have genuinely just come into existence, then this is legitimate and there is nothing for it but to repeat the exercise. Otherwise, any conditions now imposed could and should have been considered when the specification of the problem was first drawn up. This is the duty of the manager posing the problem.

The restraints may be due to either physical or conceptual conditions. Physical restraints are set, for example, by capacity limitations of factories to produce, or warehouses to store, or by the hours that staff can work. Conceptual restraints arise from the attitudes or desires of those who are going to use the solution. The farmer sets the nutritional standards he is looking for in the cattle-food he buys, or the manufacturer tries to foresee what features in his product are likely to appeal. The maker of patent medicines has his ideas on what should be the properties it possesses. All of them, however, must define the restraints in quantitative terms.

If the relationships are still linear, then the techniques of linear programming are still applicable, though not the relatively simple ones used for the two types of allocation problems. In this case the technique most commonly used is known as simplex which is both of general application and powerful, though often requiring considerable computation. As numeracy requires, the framework in which the problem is set is immaterial. This may, as in the illustrations already given, be a manufacturing framework. It may equally well be a case of preparing a salesman's journey schedule, or a matter of deciding on how to spread an advertising appropriation over a range of possible media. All these are fundamentally the same problem to be tackled in the same analytical way. The statement of the problem in fundamental terms is, as before, to find that pattern of allocating a set of facilities to meet a set of needs which will produce the greatest efficiency according to a defined measure. Now, however, any solution which does not satisfy a set of stated conditions is not considered.

The use of the technique, in most situations which will occur, is a matter for the expert, but a simple example will be worked out in order to show the reasoning which enables each successive trial made to produce usually a better and at least as good a solution as the previous one. It will also make clear how it is possible to know for certain that no better solution is possible. The problem will be considered in a semi-generalized form which can be adapted to suit any particular framework as occasion demands.

The problem tackled in the following example is trivial, and no use would be made of linear programming in practice to solve it. However, an explanation of the technique, if applied to the type of problem normally solved in this way, would involve unnecessary detail and, since the purpose is to explain the principles, the steps shown are kept to the essentials. The same principles are applied to more important examples where solutions are not obvious by inspection.

Consider 100 units of some facility which is required to meet three needs X, Y and Z. The measure of return to be obtained from allotting a unit of the facility to each of these needs is

3 per unit for X

4 per unit for Y

5 per unit for Z.

If no restrictions are imposed, then the greatest return would come by allotting all the units of the facility to meet the need Z. However, it is laid down that:

1 at least 50 units of the facility must be allotted to X, and
2 there must be not more than 30 allotted to either Y or Z.

The problem now is to discover how the facility should be allocated to produce the maximum return subject to the conditions. Merely by inspection one can see that the solution is

50 allocated to X

20 allocated to Y

30 allocated to Z

and that the return for this allocation will be 380.

Starting from any trial solution which meets the conditions, the analysis must lead to the same result.

The problem must first be stated in mathematical language.

Let x be the amount allocated to X with a return of 3 per unit

     y be the amount allocated to Y with a return of 4 per unit

     z be the amount allocated to Z with a return of 5 per unit

x, y and z must either be zero or positive, since in this type of problem negative allocations cannot be contemplated. The fact that there are 100 units to allocate is translated as $x+y+z = 100$.

The restraints that are imposed must also be expressed in mathematical terms. The first of these states that at least 50 units must be allocated to meet need X. The value of x, therefore, may be 50 or any number greater than 50. So, if p is some other unknown quantity

$$x-p = 50.$$

p may be zero, of course, but it may be any number greater than zero which conforms to the other conditions.

By similar reasoning, the other conditions can be written as

$$y+q = 30$$

and
$$z+r = 30$$

It may appear that further complications have been introduced into the problem by bringing in even more unknown quantities, p, q and r. The reason for doing so is that the conditions were originally expressed in the form of inequalities, namely x must be greater than or equal to 50, and y or z must be less than or equal to 30. Unfortunately, however, there are not very many well-understood rules of mathematical grammar for dealing with inequalities. To make the mathematical analysis easier, it is better to turn the inequalities into statements of equality, even if this means introducing apparently unnecessary further uncertainties. It remains to define the measure to be used in assessing solutions. This is the objective function which in this case is the return obtainable from the allocation pattern. Expressed mathematically, it is $A = 3x+4y+5z$. The solution that is being sought is the one which makes A as large as possible.

The mathematical problem, then, is to maximize the expression $3x+4y+5z$, subject to the conditions

$$x+y+z = 100$$
$$x-p = 50$$
$$y+q = 30$$
$$z+r = 30$$

Linear programming is, as has been stated, a trial and error method. The starting point is arbitrarily chosen as any allocation which meets the conditions. Consider an allocation in which 70 units of the facility are allocated to need X and 30 units to need Y, while no units are allocated to need Z. That is,

$$x = 70$$
$$y = 30$$
$$z = 0$$

This satisfies the condition $x+y+z = 100$. Also x is greater than 50, and y and z are not greater than 30. So this solution satisfies the conditions laid down. From these conditions it can be deduced that $p = 20$, $q = 0$ and $r = 50$. So the solution in full is:

$$x = 70 \qquad\qquad p = 20$$
$$y = 30 \qquad\qquad q = 0$$
$$z = 0 \qquad\qquad r = 30.$$

The return that comes from this allocation will be

$$(3 \times 70) + (4 \times 30) + (5 \times 0) = 330.$$

The question to be asked is whether 330 is the most that can be expected.

At the moment two of the six variables have not been brought into the solution. They are z and q, both of which have zero values. If a way could be found of discovering whether bringing them into the solution would improve it, then this would be a guide as to what the next trial should be.

To find this out, it is necessary first of all to express the values that are in the present solution in terms of those that are not. By algebra, this is found to be

$$y = 30 - q$$
$$r = 30 - z$$
$$x = 70 + q - z$$
$$p = 20 + q - z.$$

The measure for assessing the value of the solutions is $A = 3x + 4y + 5z$. x and y in this expression should now be replaced by

$$x = 70 + q - z$$

and

$$y = 30 - q$$

as developed above.

If this is done, the measure of assessment becomes $A = 330 - q + 2z$. In the present solution q and z are both zero, so A becomes 330 as before. But what would happen if q and z were given numerical values instead of being left as zero? q has a minus sign in front of it, so any value given to q would have the effect of making A less than it was before. With z it is a different story. There is a plus sign in front of it, so any value given to z must increase the value of A. The next trial should therefore include an allocation to Z. This is merely the mathematical way of stating what, in this example, is the obvious fact that the first solution contained no allocation to the need which gives the biggest return, and that the solution would be improved if it did.

In this new trial z can be given any value and clearly it would be right to make it as large as possible consistent with the conditions that have to be satisfied. It ought, therefore, to be given the value 30, but in order to illustrate the process of the analysis further, its value in this trial will be restricted to 20.

The introduction of a new value produces consequential changes in some of the other values, because all the values must conform to the conditions. For example, if y is maintained at 30 and z is now given the value 20, x must be reduced to 50 because $x+y+z = 100$. When all the changes have been worked out, the values for this trial become

$$x = 50, y = 30, z = 20, p = 0, q = 0, r = 10.$$

This gives

$$A = (3 \times 50) + (4 \times 30) + (5 \times 20)$$
$$= 370.$$

The question again arises, is this the largest return that can be achieved? As before, the variables for which values have been allotted must be expressed in terms of the variables which have zero values, and the new expressions substituted in $A = 3x+4y+5z$. If this is done, A becomes

$$370+q-2p.$$

Giving a value to q will enable A to be increased above 370. Let q be 10. Working out the consequential changes, this gives the following solution:

$$x = 50, y = 20, z = 30, p = 0, q = 10, r = 0$$
$$\text{and a value for } A = 380.$$

Following the same testing procedure, the expression for A becomes $A = 380-p-r$. Now there are only minus signs in front of the variables and therefore there is no possibility of improving the solution any further. The largest possible return is 380 and the pattern of allocation which will produce it is to allocate

50 units to need X
20 units to need Y
30 units to need Z.

Once the solution has been obtained, the other variables p, q and r can be ignored. They were only introduced in order to enable a known form of analysis to be used. They have no significance in the result.

The use of the technique provides two things:

1 a guide as to how to proceed with further trials;
2 a clear indication of when it is not possible to improve the solution any further. It must be remembered that there may be other solutions which are just as good.

Forms of the technique other than the one described here exist, but all share the common features just mentioned.

The techniques of linear programming, as has been said, are applicable when the relationships are linear. There are a sufficient number of situations in business where such relationships exist to make the technique of real value. As has been mentioned, many of these occur in the fields of transport and distribution of goods. Other examples occur in:

> Rationalization of production
> Fixing of pricing and discount policies
> Evaluation of tenders
> Formulation of investment policies
> Preparation of diets
> Devising of recipes
> Blending of products
> Reduction of trimming loss
> Preparation of duty rosters
> Production scheduling.

Such a list is, however, by no means exhaustive.

In simple cases with only two or three variables, graphical methods can be used. Beyond three variables, however, visual representations have to give place to a conceptual approach and the methods of analysis have to be employed.

Similar techniques can be employed in certain cases where the relationships are not linear. For instance, the profitability per unit of a product may not be constant, but may depend on the amounts produced. If it is of the form $k - ax$, where k is a constant and a is a constant multiplying factor applied to the level of production, then the actual profit will be $(k - ax)x$. Consider the problem when there are three products 1, 2 and 3 where the unit profits are each of this form. The total profit will be

$$P = (k_1 - a_1 x_1)x_1 + (k_2 - a_2 x_2)x_2 + (k_3 - a_3 x_3)x_3.$$

This is not a linear expression since, when multiplied out, it includes the terms $-a_1 x_1^2$, $-a_2 x_2^2$, $-a_3 x_3^2$, all of which are second degree terms. Suppose each product contains the same three ingredients. The recipes will give the quantity of each ingredient for each unit of output for each product.

Suppose these are as given in the following table:

| | Products | | |
| | 1 | 2 | 3 |
Ingredient	(Qty. x_1)	(Qty. x_2)	(Qty. x_3)
1	2	3	4
2	1	2	3
3	3	4	5

Then the totals used will be

$$\text{Ingredient 1:} \quad 2x_1 + 3x_2 + 4x_3$$
$$\text{Ingredient 2:} \quad x_1 + 2x_2 + 3x_3$$
$$\text{Ingredient 3:} \quad 3x_1 + 4x_2 + 5x_3$$

The conditions laid down may be supposed to be that the quantity available of ingredient one is q_1, of ingredient two is q_2, and of ingredient three is q_3.
Then

$$2x_1 + 3x_2 + 4x_3 \text{ must not be greater than } q_1$$
$$x_1 + 2x_2 + 3x_3 \text{ must not be greater than } q_2$$
$$3x_1 + 4x_2 + 5x_3 \text{ must not be greater than } q_3$$

$$P = (k_1 - a_1 x_1)x_1 + (k_2 - a_2 x_2)x_2 + (k_3 - a_3 x_3)x_3$$

The problem is to find values of output x_1, x_2 and x_3 which will make P as large as possible, subject to the limiting conditions laid down by the availability of materials. It will be noticed that this is the same form of problem as that tackled by linear programming, except that the objective function is quadratic and not linear. This type of problem can be solved by a very similar technique to the one used in linear relationships. When it is not appropriate, then techniques which are not in the least similar to linear programming have to be used. Some of these will be described in the section dealing with problems of strategy.

Another class of problem arises when the needs to be met are not constant during the period which is being studied. If the rate at which the needs arise is uniform, the problem of deciding on the facilities to be provided is capable of straightforward solution. If the needs arise randomly, the matter of deciding on the facilities to provide is not so straightforward. The needs to be met form a queue awaiting service, and the waiting time for members of the queue provides the key to the solution.

One example of queues occurs at a petrol filling station. A queue of cars forms to await service and this queue will vary in length. A second queue, consisting of the unused facilities of petrol pumps and other attendants, will fluctuate in length throughout the same period. The lengths of these two queues will change in opposite directions. As the queue of unserved cars increases, the queue of unused facilities diminishes, and vice versa. It would be possible to make either queue as small as one liked at the expense of causing the other to grow correspondingly. Both queues are going to give rise to penalties. Motorists who have to wait too long for attention decide to wait no longer, or may wait on this occasion but decide to go elsewhere in the future. A queue of unused facilities incurs direct costs in the shape of the unused investment in equipment and also wages paid to attendants who have nothing to do. The problem consists of deciding on how the queues should be balanced so that the combined penalties are as small as possible.

The problem is again a universal one. Further examples occur in providing a number of check-out points in a self-service store to serve the needs of customers waiting to pay for their purchases, counter attendants in post offices or bank tellers at bank counters, or in providing dustcarts and dustmen to collect dustbins, to name a few. All these are examples of exactly the same problem—a waiting time problem.

Waiting time problems may involve people, objects, abstract activities or a combination of these. In any queueing situation one can identify as the elements:

1 the unit which has a need to be met;
2 the facility which has a service to offer;
3 the service which is offered by the facility.

In a parking situation, for instance, the unit facility is the parking space available and the service offered is parking time. A machine broken down has maintenance men offering repair time. At a seaport, ships look for berths where unloading or loading equipment is offered. The earliest development of a theory to handle queueing problems occurred in connection with telephone exchanges in 1908. In that year A. K. Erland, on the staff of the Copenhagen Telephone Company, was involved in finding an answer to the question of how much relay equipment should be provided to deal with the expected subscriber traffic. Too much equipment provided would mean unnecessary capital tied up, while too little would mean dissatisfied customers, a bad image and insufficient expansion of the business. To settle this question, he began to study the characteristics of queues and the way they could be expected to behave under certain conditions.

In order to analyse a queueing problem the basic characteristics of the queue must first be measured. These are:

1 The input of the units which have needs to be met, and here what is of interest is the pattern of their arrivals. This can be measured by specifying either the frequency of arrival of the units or the time that elapses between two successive arrivals. This is not enough information, however. It is necessary also to know how these arrivals are distributed over the period. Are they spread uniformly, occurring at equal intervals, for instance? Are they occurring in entirely random fashion? Whatever is the pattern it can be described by a frequency distribution or a mathematical expression.

2 The service provided. Again, measurement and information on the rate at which the service is provided and the pattern of its availability is needed.

3 The rules governing the behaviour of the queue itself. Is it a question of first come first served? Are there any rules for giving priority, like ladies first? What is the degree of priority that can be claimed—the right to be served after the service to the present recipient is finished or pre-emptive, or the right to displace the present recipient before the service is completed and claim service instead? These definitions of the queue discipline must be the responsibility of the manager.

A self-service store with a single check-out point is an example of a queueing situation. Suppose the average rate of arrival of customers at the check-out point is 90 every hour and the cashier on average deals with 120 customers every hour. In this case

the measure of input is $90/60 = 1 \cdot 5$ customers per minute
the measure of service is $120/60 = 2 \cdot 0$ customers per minute

The ratio of these two measures is important. In this case

$$\frac{\text{measure of input}}{\text{measure of service}} = \frac{1 \cdot 5}{2 \cdot 0} = 0 \cdot 75$$

This ratio is known as the traffic density and is denoted by ρ. It is of interest to note that this is independent of the time unit used. Other symbols customarily used are λ to denote the measure of input and μ to denote the measure of service.

The traffic density gives a guide as to whether the queue is likely to be manageable. If it is less than 1 and the measure of input and the measure of service both do not vary, then the queue situation is a steady one. If the traffic density is greater than 1 or equal to 1, then the queue situation will become unstable and, even as it approaches 1, there will be an increasing probability of there being a long queue.

If the pattern of arrivals at the check-out point is known to be a random one, then using probability theory, it is possible to obtain answers to a number of important questions. There is more than one type of random arrival pattern. One such is known as a Poisson distribution. It represents a situation in which the probability of an arrival is constant and is not influenced either by the time of the arrival or by the state of the queueing system at that time. Assumptions have also to be made regarding the number of service channels, and whether any but random influences affect the completion of service for any one unit arriving in the system. For a system in which arrivals are of Poisson type and service completions are random, formulae can be derived as follows:

$$\text{average number of units in the queue} = \frac{\rho^2}{1-\rho}$$

$$\text{average waiting time} = \frac{\rho}{\mu - \lambda}$$

(λ = measure of input, μ = measure of service).

The answers to these questions can be expressed only in terms of probability and averages, since the data from which they are deduced is itself expressible only in terms of probabilities. This does not mean that the value of the results is small, so long as there is an understanding of the methods of handling probability.

In the case of the check-out example mentioned above

$$\lambda = 1\cdot5$$
$$\mu = 2\cdot0$$
$$\rho = 0\cdot75$$

and so one can deduce, amongst other things, that

1 the average number of people in the queue will be

$$(\tfrac{3}{4})^2 \div (1-\tfrac{3}{4}) = \tfrac{3}{4} \times \tfrac{3}{4} \div \tfrac{1}{4} = 2\tfrac{1}{4}$$

2 the average waiting time will be

$$\tfrac{3}{4} \div (2-\tfrac{1}{2}) = \tfrac{3}{4} \div \tfrac{1}{2} = 1\tfrac{1}{2} \text{ minutes}$$

These are statistical averages. They do not mean that the queue is always of either two or three people. The queue may at any one time contain any number of people. What they do mean, however, is that the consequences to the manager of the behaviour of all the varying lengths of queues over a period of time is the same as if he were faced with a constant queue of two to three people, each of whom has to wait for one and a half minutes.

As always, careful attention has to be paid to the specification of the characteristics of the problem. In particular, in dealing with queue situations a distinction has to be made between those who are delayed before servicing begins and the number of those who are in the system as a whole. This latter number includes those who are already being serviced and who will therefore not have to wait for the full servicing time before emerging from the system. The queue proper can be defined as those who have to wait before their servicing can begin.

With due attention to these distinctions, formulae can be derived to enable values to be calculated for, for instance, the probability that a queue exists, the probability that there will be more than n units in the queue and the probability that any unit needs to wait for service.

With a knowledge of these formulae the effect of changes in the pace of business can be forecast. Suppose, for instance, the value of λ became 1·9. That is, the average rate of arrivals goes up to

114 per hour, while there is no change in the rate at which the check-out operates. Now

$$\lambda = 1\cdot9$$
$$\mu = 2\cdot0$$
$$\rho = 0\cdot95$$

The new values of some of the characteristics of the store situation are shown as follows contrasted with the old.

Rate of arrivals	90 an hour	114 an hour
Average number in queue	2–3	18–19
Average waiting time	$1\frac{1}{2}$ minutes	$9\frac{1}{12}$ minutes

It will be noticed at once that in this situation a relatively modest increase of twenty-four persons an hour in the activity has brought about a striking change, both in the average length of the queue and the average amount of time that any one person will have to wait. If activity further increased, the congestion at the check-out point would grow at an increasing rate. So long as the average arrival rate remains less than the average service rate the situation remains controllable, but likely to result in considerable dissatisfaction. Once, however, the average arrival rate becomes the same as the average service rate, the average length of queue will be infinitely large and the situation becomes unstable and out of hand. This is because the arrival rates of the customers are distributed round both sides of the average, and unfortunately time gained when the rates are favourable and customers are widely spaced cannot be stored up for later use when arrival rates are unfavourable and customers are coming in thick and fast.

Exactly the same queueing situations can arise in the handling of stocks and in the balancing of successive stages of a manufacturing process where, not infrequently, a good balance is considered just the right thing to achieve. At first sight it is attractive to have a nicely balanced service rate and arrival rate. However, the analysis shows that, unless the arrival rate can be rigidly controlled so that it never varies, there will always be a queue, and that in these circumstances, the nearer the average rates of arrival and service come to each other, the greater will be the risk of congestion and instability.

A manager will often sense this instinctively and express it to himself in terms of having insufficient margin in case of accidents. If he is numerate, his instinct is confirmed but, more important, he is able to have measured for him the degree of risk and the cost of the steps necessary to guard against any particular level of risk. This is the value of applying this particular technique.

The example that has been considered earlier was a Poisson type of distribution with no limits set on the input or the number allowed into the system, and with one single service channel serving one unit at a time. It is not to be supposed, however, that these are the only conditions that can apply, or that analysis cannot deal with other groups of characteristics.

In particular, variations from this basic situation, although they may not all apply to, say, a self-service store, may consist of:

1 multiple channels instead of single channels of service;
2 other types of arrival pattern. In the one considered so far the probability of an arrival was constant and was not influenced either by the time of the arrival or by the state of the queueing system at that time. Other forms of arrival and service patterns assume that these restrictions are removed;
3 patterns of arrival where a limit is put on the size of the queue that is allowed;
4 patterns of service where the probability of service being completed at any instant is not independent of the time when service began. This is the type of distribution of servicing on which Erland worked out his original theories for the telephone;
5 patterns of service where more than one channel of service is allowed in parallel;
6 various rules for giving priority treatment to certain classes of queue members. These may be for social reasons or to improve efficiency.

For the examples and the deviations considered, there are methods of mathematical analysis that can be used to solve problems that conform to one or other of the patterns.

All the approaches to solving waiting time problems depend on it being possible to express the data in some recognizable mathematical form and to apply accepted techniques of mathematical analysis. Sometimes, however, the data defies any such approach. Nevertheless, it is not necessary to abandon hope of arriving at any worthwhile conclusions from it. Even if there is no recognized mathematical representation of the situation, it may still be possible to devise a logical model of the situation. This may then obviate a decision to build a physical pilot plant for a proposed development. One obvious disadvantage for the latter course is that it may not be possible to reproduce in a pilot plant all the conditions that will apply in the larger situation. Another is that building physical models is a costly business. Even if these two objections are not present, there may still remain the disadvantage that the only physical pilot model possible is to introduce the full-size operation, but in stages, with a possible consequent need to reverse the operation at a later stage. To decide physically how many further check-out points are desirable in a self-service store cannot be done by reproducing the activity in miniature, but only by trying the full-size operation in stages and introducing first one and then another check-out point, always being ready to remove one if it is found at any stage that there are too many. Can all these disadvantages be overcome by simulating the situations at the mental level instead of the physical level? The attempt to do so in general is known as simulation. The advantages of the successful use of simulation techniques are great. Not only can very many more modifications to the system be considered, but this can be done to a much greater degree of sophistication and at a very much smaller cost than if done physically. Moreover, simulation studies need not involve any particular mathematical relationships. These can sometimes lead to formulae which, though correct, are impracticable to evaluate.

In the particular instance of finding solutions to waiting time problems, a technique known as Monte Carlo can be employed. The name Monte Carlo, with its overtones of chance, is the simulation technique which is applicable to situations where the relationships have to be expressed in terms of probabilities. Consider, for example, a barber's shop. At the moment there is only one chair with the proprietor doing the work himself. Business is brisk and the proprietor is considering installing a second chair and employing an assistant. This, however, for a small business is a step not to be taken lightly, and he does not wish to incur the expense without being reasonably satisfied that it is worth doing. How can he set about finding out?

First he must be sure what the present situation really is. Observation carried out methodically and over a period will establish for him what the pattern of arrivals of his customers is on most occasions. On any one day the pattern will certainly be different from this most probable pattern, and indeed no one day may ever be exactly the same as another. However, if the day be divided up into periods of a quarter of an hour, or ten minutes, or five minutes, or whatever the proprietor considers the best interval to distinguish the detail, a pattern will emerge. Customers have varying needs, some taking up five minutes of the barber's time, another perhaps twenty minutes. This pattern too needs to be identified. Both patterns can conveniently be expressed as percentage frequency distributions.

For example, for five minute intervals the figures might be:

Observed Activity

Arrivals per interval	No. of Cases	% Frequency
0	120	24
1	160	32
2	130	26
3	70	14
4	20	4

Servicing Times in Minutes	No. of Cases	% Frequency
5	40	8
7	190	38
9	150	30
11	50	10
13	30	6
15	20	4
17	20	4

This then is the data of the situation. How to represent it adequately is the next question, and to answer it one must look for a situation where random occurrences happen with a pattern of frequency as shown in the table above.

To simulate this a selection of 100 numbers running from 00 to 99 must be provided and allocated to represent the happenings accurately. This allocation is as follows:

Arrivals	% Frequency	Allocated Numbers
0	24	00–23
1	32	24–55
2	26	56–81
3	14	82–95
4	4	96–99

F

Servicing Times	% Frequency	Allocated Numbers
5	8	00–07
7	38	08–45
9	30	46–75
11	10	76–85
13	6	86–91
15	4	92–95
17	4	96–99

The randomness of the happenings must now be simulated. This can be done in a number of ways. The numbers may consist of discs or tickets placed in a hat from which they are drawn blindfold, being returned to the hat after each drawing. This is important because there must always be a full selection of numbers, so that there is always an equal chance of each being drawn. Another method of providing random chance is to generate a set of random numbers from a mathematical formula. This is tedious by hand, but rapidly done using a computer. Every month a set of random numbers is produced by Ernie, for instance, in drawing Premium Bonds. Tables of previously generated random numbers can also be purchased.

The apparatus is now ready and the exercise can proceed. One number is drawn from one set of the random numbers and then replaced. This represents the number of customers who arrive for the first period. This is found by consulting the frequency table. Suppose it is found that this first number represents 2 customers. From the set of random numbers representing the service times, 2 numbers must be drawn, since there are 2 customers. These numbers are replaced immediately. Suppose they are found to represent a service time of 5 minutes and 11 minutes respectively. At the commencement of the day both chairs are empty, so each customer gets immediate attention. The first chair will be occupied for five minutes and the second chair for eleven minutes. This is shown diagrammatically in Figure 6, and for simplicity customers are assumed to arrive at the beginning of the period.

Now consider the second period. A drawing from the arrivals hat may show 3 customers A, B and C arriving, and their service times are found to be 5 minutes for A, 5 minutes for B and 7 minutes for C. At the beginning of this 5 minute period, however, only the first chair is empty. Customer A gets immediate attention, but

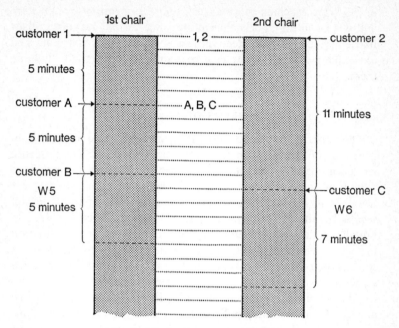

FIG. 6.—The barber and Monte Carlo.

customers *B* and *C* will have to wait. From the diagram one sees
that the first chair will again be empty before the second chair, and
customer *B* now gets attention having waited five minutes. Customer
C, however, has to wait a further 1 minute until the second chair is
free. His wait therefore has lasted 6 minutes. In the first 10 minutes
the total customer waiting time is 11 minutes.

So the exercise continues and the most probable total customer
waiting time can be found. Equally, of course, there is a chance as
shown in the table that no customers will enter. This may result in
a chair remaining empty. From the same diagram the most likely
chair utilization can be found. The manager has something to go on
now and can make his decision without having to go to the length
of installing a second chair and engaging an assistant only to find
perhaps it was not justified.

Using a computer, many weeks or months of experience can be
followed through quite quickly. Much more complex situations
than the one just considered can be simulated on paper and the
consequences of various possible changes in procedures worked out

in this way. Machine shop set-ups, refinery operations, production and stock control models have all been successfully set up and their likeliest outcomes predicted. Industrial wars, in a much more real sense than military wars, can be won without actually fighting them.

PROBLEMS OF STRATEGY

The types of problems hitherto considered have ranged from problems of identification to waiting time problems. The sequence has been one in which the data has become less and less certain in definition. In all of them, however, it was assumed that the way the elements in the situation would behave or react after a decision would be affected only by the decision taken. This, however, is not always the case. Sometimes a new factor enters into the situation in the shape of an uncontrollable reaction of some of the elements to the type of decision taken. This will normally be the case where some of the elements are themselves decision-makers with a power to take action in response to an initial decision of one's own. Thus, in deciding on marketing policies it is necessary to take into account not only the likeliest outcomes for the actions that the decision-maker can take, but also how these outcomes can be modified by all the possible actions of competitors and the various likelihoods of these possible actions.

The situation is akin to a game of cards and mathematical techniques which can be used to help in reaching solutions of problems of this sort are classified as a theory of games. They can be applied where certain characteristics of the situation are clear. It must be known how many parties there are able to make their own decisions, and also what courses of action are open to each, but not which of them will be chosen. It is further necessary that the gains or losses which will accrue to each of the parties should depend on the actions of each and that there are rules by which these gains or losses can be calculated. The theory of games provides a means by which the strategies which each of the parties should employ can be discovered if each chooses to operate always to his best advantage.

The simplest example of this type of situation is when two parties directly oppose each other, and each is trying to gain as much as possible at the expense of the other. In a sales situation, if the market cannot be expanded, what increase in the share of the market is obtained by one of the only two companies operating in it is balanced by the loss of market share sustained by the other. Since the sum of the gains and the losses must necessarily be zero, these games are called two person zero sum games.

Suppose, for example, two companies X and Y at the moment share the market equally, and that if they both continue their existing methods of sales promotion there is no reason to suppose that this situation would change. Both companies have open to them the possibility of either introducing a premium gift scheme or sponsoring sports competitions, but not of doing both, and the costs of operating either scheme is virtually the same for both companies. Company X has three possible strategies open to it, and for each of these Company Y has three possible strategies. There are, therefore, nine possible situations and nine possible ways in which the market shares can alter. These can be examined.

It is reliably estimated that the following changes in market share will occur according to the different courses of action followed.

X does nothing and Y does nothing	X gains 0%
	Y loses 0%
X sponsors a sports competition and	X gains 10%
Y does nothing	Y loses 10%
X introduces premium gifts and	X gains 30%
Y does nothing	Y loses 30%
X does nothing and Y sponsors a sports	X loses 10%
competition	Y gains 10%
X sponsors a sports competition and	X gains 0%
Y sponsors a sports competition	Y loses 0%
X introduces premium gifts and Y	X gains 15%
sponsors a sports competition	Y loses 15%
X does nothing and Y introduces premium	X loses 25%
gifts	Y gains 25%
X sponsors a sports competition and Y	X loses 10%
introduces premium gifts	Y gains 10%
X introduces premium gifts and Y	X gains 5%
introduces premium gifts	Y loses 5%

These gains and losses are more easily compared when seen in tabular form. Such a table is known as a pay off matrix. The pay off matrix for this situation is as follows, showing X's gains as plus and X's losses as minus.

Company X	Company Y		
	Does nothing	Sponsors a sports competition	Introduces premium gifts
Does nothing	0	−10	−25
Sponsors a sports competition	+10	0	−10
Introduces premium gifts	+30	+15	+5

A pay off matrix for Y's gains and losses would have the same figures as above, but with plus and minus signs interchanged.

X clearly has the edge over Y in the matter of introducing premium gifts, perhaps because X has made arrangements with a specialist company while Y is making its own arrangements. The right course of action for X is to introduce premium gifts, because by doing so there is a gain whatever strategy Y adopts. What, however, should Y's strategy be in the circumstances?

If Y's director of marketing had made no attempt to measure the situation in quantitative terms and merely knew that X had the edge over him in the matter of premium gifts, he would certainly deduce that the strategy X would follow would be to introduce premium gifts. He might well react to this by considering that he should at all costs do something different from X to provide a contrast. If, however, he has available to him the estimates in the table, then it will be clear to him that his correct course of action is to introduce premium gifts also. In this way he will keep as low as possible the gain which X is certain to get. Y's director of marketing will eventually have to set up a new situation or go out of business, but for the time being he has to do the best he can, and using the theory of games will show him what it is he should do.

In mathematical terms the situation is known as a game. The solution involved only one course of action throughout. Both X and Y followed a pure strategy. Looking at the table again, it will be noticed that the lowest figures of each of the rows, counting all negative figures as lower than all positive figures, are −25, −10 and +5. The largest of these is +5. At the same time the highest figures of each of the columns are +30, +15 and +5. The smallest of these is +5. In this case the largest of the row minima and the smallest of the column maxima are the same, and the game is said to have a saddle point. The solution is known as a minimax solution and the game itself is said to have the value +5.

If there is no saddle point, then a pure strategy will not result in the maximum return. Both participants must mix their strategies, now choosing one strategy and now another. The theory of games can be used to discover in what proportions different strategies should be used.

Not all game situations are two person zero sum. In a marketing situation it is more often the case than not that the market is capable of expansion, and that one person's gains are not solely at the expense of another. Moreover, to have only two participants would be the exception rather than the rule, and the number of courses of action available to the participants is not necessarily the same for all. Variations of the technique used for the simple game have in some cases been worked out for other game situations. When the game situation is man v. nature, a special treatment has to be employed. The mistake must be avoided of investing nature with personality and assuming that she will pick her strategies following the same rules as one's own. For business decision-making, some progress is possible by assuming first that nature will be at her worst and evaluating the results on that assumption. Then assuming that nature is in her most benevolent mood, a second lot of results can be compared with the first. This will, at the very least, establish the outcome of the extreme strategies that are possible.

When there are many participants, progress can be made by considering a series of games in which various consortia compete against each other. Consider, for example, four competing firms P, Q, R and S. It is always open to any of the firms to contemplate forming a consortium with one or more of its present competitors, so there are seven possible games to be considered:

$$P \text{ v. } Q, R \text{ and } S$$
$$Q \text{ v. } R, S \text{ and } P$$
$$R \text{ v. } S, P \text{ and } Q$$
$$S \text{ v. } P, Q \text{ and } R$$
$$PQ \text{ v. } RS$$
$$PR \text{ v. } QS$$
$$PS \text{ v. } QR$$

Each of the companies will have a view of the minimum benefit it is prepared to accept either by staying on its own or by joining in a consortium. A solution to the main game would be one which produced a set of benefits which exceeded the minimum for each of the companies, and the strategies adopted by each company would be based on the consortia which appeared in the solution.

Pay-off tables can be constructed for much more complex problem situations than those discussed so far. However, the information contained in a pay-off table can be presented in an alternative manner, which in complex decision situations can lead to more complete understanding. This is to present it in the form of a decision tree, which not only shows the values of all the possible outcomes but the analysis by which these values are obtained. To do so it is necessary to investigate three factors relating to each of all the possible outcomes—the likelihood of each outcome, the satisfaction to be obtained from each, and the length of time which will elapse before the satisfaction is obtained.

Consider an organization whose aim is to bring out a new product. Two major policy decisions have to be taken.

First it has to decide between developing its own new product and buying one, perhaps by taking over a company. This decision is followed by a second decision between using the same marketing policy as before or devising a new one.

These choices can be shown diagrammatically as in Figure 7.

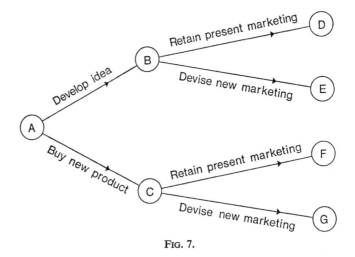

FIG. 7.

Point *A* is the present moment of decision and either point *B* or point *C* will be the second moment of decision. Depending on which pair of choices is made, one of four situations will ensue. These are shown as points *D, E, F* or *G*.

The four routes by which one or other of these situations is reached are:

1 To develop a new product and to market it by existing methods.
2 To develop a new product and to devise a new marketing plan.
3 To buy a new product and to market it by existing methods.
4 To buy a new product and to devise a new marketing plan.

The satisfaction to be obtained from the outcomes arising from each of these situations must now be measured. The future business likely to result if the organization finds itself in each of the four situations is estimated. This will be done by using any estimating methods considered appropriate and making full use of the knowledge, experience and judgement of the marketing leadership.

Suppose that the measures of these outcome satisfactions are respectively:

1 £120,000
2 £100,000
3 £90,000
4 £100,000

When these are inserted the diagram becomes as follows (Figure 8).

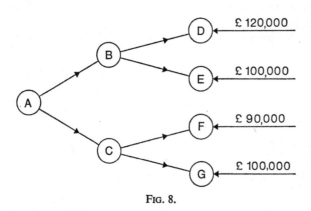

£ 120,000
£ 100,000
£ 90,000
£ 100,000

Fig. 8.

The decision-maker, ignoring the lapse of time between decision and outcome and assuming equal chances of successfully implementing his decisions has no difficulty in making his choice. The satisfaction of £120,000 points to the pair of decisions requiring the development of a new product to be marketed by existing methods.

How realistic is it to assume that all decisions have an equal chance of being successfully implemented? This must depend on the circumstances of individual problems. In every case, however, where no attempt is made to measure the chances of success, the assumption is being made, even though by default, that the chances are equal.

The statement of the problem is incomplete without estimates of probabilities and their insertion into the picture adds a new factor for consideration which may lead to a different decision. Suppose in this problem the following chances of success are estimated:

Activity	Chance of Success
Develop new product	70%
Buy a new product	90%
Obtain a satisfactory response by the public to the new product using existing marketing plan	60%
Obtain a satisfactory response by the public to the new product using a new marketing plan	80%

Here again, it is the expertise of the line managers which is needed where these estimates of success are made. As always in numerate decision-making, it is at this stage of formulating the problem that experience and judgement are necessary.

Figure 9 shows the diagram when these probabilities are inserted.

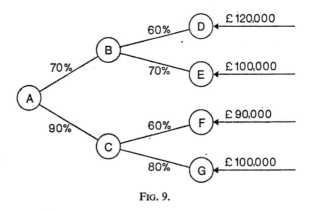

Fig. 9.

What requires to be deduced are probabilities of reaching each of the four ultimate situations. To make this deduction, recourse has to be made to the rules provided by the theory of probability.

The probability of reaching situation D is the probability of successfully developing a new product multiplied by the probability of obtaining a satisfactory response by the public to the new product using the existing marketing plan.

A 70% chance of success implies a probability of $\dfrac{70}{100}$

A 60% chance of success implies a probability of $\dfrac{60}{100}$

Hence the probability of reaching situation D is

$$\frac{70}{100} \times \frac{60}{100} = \frac{42}{100}$$

Similarly,

the probability of reaching situation E is $\dfrac{49}{100}$

the probability of reaching situation F is $\dfrac{54}{100}$

the probability of reaching situation G is $\dfrac{72}{100}$

The pay-off for a situation is the satisfaction of that situation multiplied by the probability of that satisfaction being enjoyed.

The pay-off for D is

$$£120,000 \times \frac{42}{100} = £50,400$$

Similarly,

the pay-off for E is £49,000
the pay-off for F is £48,600
the pay-off for G is £72,000

Figure 10 shows the diagram when the satisfactions are replaced by pay-offs.

The details may now be omitted since the pay-off figures combine the measures of probability and satisfaction for every element in the configuration. The decision-maker's thinking may now be directed to the effects of both chance of success and satisfaction on the situations which may result instead of the satisfactions alone.

If point B has already been reached, the comparison between the pay-offs at D and E provides a basis for the decision at that point and would influence the decision-makers towards the choice of

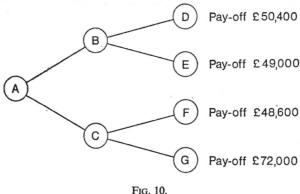

FIG. 10.

continuing with existing market plans. In this way the higher pay-off of £50,400 at *D* would be attained. Similarly, if point *C* has already been reached the higher pay-off at *G* would be attained by adopting a new marketing plan.

At point *A* the decision required, on the other hand, lies between developing a new product and buying a new product. One argument on which the decision might be based is that the highest of the ultimate pay-offs arises from being in situation *G*. In order to provide the chance of being in that situation the decision at point *A* must be to buy a new product in preference to developing one. An alternative argument is based on a comparison of the pay-offs at *B* and *C*. The measure of the pay-off at *B* can be taken as the sum of the pay-offs at *D* and *E*. This is shown in Figure 11.

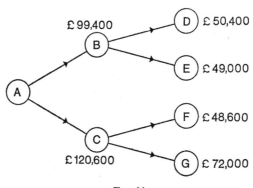

FIG. 11.

Arithmetically this is a weighted average of the satisfactions at *D* and *E*, the weighting factors being the success estimates of the activities *ABD* and *ABE*. In this example the pay-off at *B* will be £99,400. In the same way, the pay-off at *C* is calculated at £120,600. On this view, the decision would be to make the choice *AC* as providing the means of attaining the outcome with the larger pay-off. It is to be noticed that on either view, when success estimates are taken into account in this example, the decision will be to buy a new product. This is different from the decision to develop a new product, reached when only satisfaction estimates were considered.

In practice a decision tree would have many more branches, breaking up into many more smaller branches and ultimately into twigs. At the end of each twig is a golden apple and the size of each apple may be very different one from each other. The worth of each apple is undoubtedly one factor influencing the choice of decision to be made at each branching point. So too is the prospect of reaching the prize.

Allowance must also be made for differences in time. This can be done by discounting the values of the pay-offs at the end of the branches at an agreed rate of interest before summing them to give the pay-off at the branching points. Differing costs of the alternative choices can be allowed for by using net pay-off figures rather than gross.

Other factors which may affect the decision-maker are the penalties of failure and the chances of failure at various stages, the possibility or not of switching to another branch at a later stage of the strategy and the propensity of the decision-maker to take risks or to play for safety. The technique can be extended to cover all such factors.

Techniques for solving problems of strategy have been considered last in this chapter, and this for two reasons. First, strategic decision-making involves the use of probability measurement and the techniques of handling uncertainty are less widely applied as yet than others. Secondly, the measurement of probabilities is difficult. For these reasons problems of strategy have not received much general investigation except in specialized circles. The potential rewards, however, are likely to be far greater if they are correctly solved than in any other type of problem. Techniques for reaching solutions, as yet in their infancy, would repay study and development.

CHAPTER III

THE NATURE OF PROBLEMS

THE techniques discussed in the previous chapter form part of the subject of operational research. They are an aid to solving problems whose characteristics comprise a statement of a situation, a definition of the elements involved, measurements of their strengths and the posing of a question. The answer is reached by a step-by-step analysis, the technique supplying the rules of the analysis. Such problems of analysis constitute a very large category of problems that face decision-makers.

They are not, however, the only category of problems that face managers in their capacity either as decision-makers or as leaders. The final phase of the management function is action. Before action comes decision, and before decision the investigation of a problem. The start of the process is the recognition and definition of a problem.

Yet surprisingly little appears in the existing management literature regarding the nature of problems. Many management textbooks examine excellently and thoroughly the frameworks in which managements operate, given that certain solutions to the problems have been found. They also elaborate the methods by which the solutions can be translated into action. Most pay little attention to the original solution-finding processes. They also largely assume that the frameworks and methods of operation are the same irrespective of the differing nature of the problems facing the organization. Dr Peter Drucker, indeed, having in his introduction to *Managing for Results* said: 'To every executive's desk come dozens of problems every morning, all clamouring for his attention. But there is little to tell him which are important and which merely noisy', three pages later states: 'Results are obtained by exploiting opportunities, not by solving problems.' If one understands him aright, he advocates a pragmatic approach, and in terms of that approach develops his pattern of *Managing for Results*. Certainly, there is little examination of the problems that arise, and Drucker's advice is 'Resources to produce results must be allocated to opportunities rather than to problems. Needless to say, one cannot shrug off all problems, but they can and should be minimized.'

Colonel Lyndall Urwick, by contrast, in *The Pattern of Management* makes frequent reference to the use of the principles of scientific management and does examine the contrast between the practical man and the theorist in their attack on any problem. He refers, too, with approval to F. W. Taylor's pleas for a study of analogous situations and problems in industry and belief that general guiding lines and principles could be extracted from such a study which would offer a much more effective procedure than relying only on what a man could learn from his own restricted environment. Unfortunately Colonel Urwick falls short of examining the nature of the analogous situations and problems Taylor mentioned.

Rosemary Stewart goes further than most in investigating the nature of problems. In her book *The Reality of Management* she lists a number of ways in which management can improve the standard of its decision-making. Among these are included:

'By analysing decision-making in stages to make certain it has: one, formulated the reasons for taking a decision and defined the problem to be solved: two, analysed the nature of the problem: and, three, examined the alternative solutions and their possible consequences.'

The approach of this book is more in line with Rosemary Stewart than with Drucker. In this chapter the attempt is made to categorize the decision-making areas in terms of the problems involved and to define their characteristics. In particular, each is examined to see whether for each there is a need for numeracy.

Underlying and preceding any management decision is a prediction. Decisions always relate to the future. The action following from the decision will take place in an environment which is different from the present at the very least in its point of time, if in no other respect. The decision, therefore, cannot avoid accepting as its basis a prediction of what that environment is going to be. If it is a positive prediction resulting from deliberate thought, so much the better. An assumption that the decision can be based on the present state of the environment is a prediction that such changes as will occur can be ignored. The assumption may not even be explicitly made. Nevertheless, basing a decision on the present, even in default of any thought whatever concerning the future, is an implied prediction that changes will be insignificant.

More definite assumptions will result in more positive predictions and an understanding of the problems of making good predictions is of extreme importance.

PROBLEMS OF PREDICTION

The business man is not unwilling to make predictions. Like all other men he is anxious to see what the future holds for him if he can. He shares with all men the common historical background which accorded to the soothsayers and astrologers of earlier times positions of considerable importance. Like others, he ceased to listen to them, not because he judged them to be engaged in wrongful pursuits, but because he came to the conclusion that they were unsuccessful in their endeavours. Modern forecasters who produce sound predictions can be sure of an attentive audience.

Together with his inclination to look ahead, man possesses in some measure the ability to do so. In this he differs from every other member of the animal kingdom. A dog, left on its own by its master, knows only that it has been left. It may be conditioned to await patiently his return, but cannot by reasoning satisfy itself that he will return. Man in similar circumstances can do so. He alone can reason about the future from the present. He does it in many different ways and with varying degrees of efficiency.

The distinction must be drawn between short-term forecasting and long-term prediction. Where the division comes is a matter of circumstance. In an intricate heart operation, ten seconds may be a long time, whereas in a mining operation, ten years may be considered to be a very short period. One approach is to consider how long it will be before plans prepared with the intention of altering the operations of the organization are implemented. A new electricity generating station takes about six years to plan, construct and bring into operation. Periods of longer than six years, therefore, for the electricity supply industry, are long-term, and periods of less than six years are short-term.

If long-term prediction is practised along with short-term fore-casting, the two need to be related in order to achieve consistency. Both give rise to decisions which will lead to action. The principles of numeracy require that the short-term forecasts equally with the long-term predictions should take the broad view. This means that they should be made within the framework of the long-term prediction, and should not create situations which make the fulfilment of long-term predictions impossible to achieve. This is not to say that short-term forecasts may not show the need for changes in long-term predictions, but, until the changes are made, compatibility must be maintained.

The crudest of the techniques of prediction is elemental forecasting. Here the process is initiated by striking a keynote. This must be done by somebody in authority. The keynote, for example, may be

1 that forecasts are to be based on the introduction of stated new production facilities;
2 that a ten per cent or some other increase in activity is to be envisaged; or
3 that costs are to be contained within a stated increase over present costs.

Next, the requirement is broken down into a number of individual requirements dealing with a particular element of the whole. Thus, in a food manufacturing firm, the total requirement is broken down into a series of requirements for soups, baked beans, other canned foods, salad cream, tomato ketchup, other bottled goods, baby foods, squashes and so on. It is now the task of the individual in charge of the particular element to prepare his forecast for a defined period ahead. Finally, the various elemental forecasts are collected together and combined to form the total forecast.

Such a technique was very widely used until comparatively recently. It can only be successful if the keynote is accurately defined, and if the organization is in a position to ensure that it is followed exactly. This in turn requires that the elements involved in the forecast do not change their character and are largely independent of any external influences.

The principal disadvantage of this procedure arises from the fact that the forecasts are prepared independently and in isolation. The possible effects of one elemental forecast upon other elements receive scant attention. Often, too, since the initiative is directed by superior authority, the forecast becomes a description of what it is thought will please rather than an objective statement. One way to mitigate these disadvantages is to have the forecasts considered at a conference of all involved. The effect of outside influences can also be considered. Time, however, rarely permits for any broad discussion and lack of knowledge will prevent investigation in depth. Elemental forecasting tends to be an

G

interpretation rather than a forecast. Its deductions are qualitative, though often decked out in quantitative form.

The quantitative element can be introduced by employing statistical and other mathematical techniques. There are a number of ways in which this is done. Essentially they all consist of first studying the data of past events and then attempting to identify the pattern to which these events conform. It may then be possible to represent the pattern by a mathematical expression or a graph whose mathematical equation is known. The justification for this procedure is that, if this *can* be done, then employing the rules of mathematical grammar will enable the future to be predicted quantitatively.

Caution is needed. Difficulties arise when the historical data is insufficient to provide a definite pattern. Even if plentiful over the range for which the data is available, there may be more than one curve which could fit. These, though very similar for the range where data exists, would diverge in their projections forward into the future. Predictions based upon them would differ according to which curve was chosen. Again, the pattern might be one to which no standard curve could provide a good fit. In this case the form of the prediction would depend upon an arbitrary choice of the curve to fit the pattern.

The use of a mathematical curve presupposes that the pattern identified from past data is going to continue unchanged into the future. Prediction is easiest if the pattern of the data is a straight line. This represents the situation in which, as in Figure 12, the increase in value year by year is the same. Projecting the straight line forward assumes that this annual increase will continue to be the same.

Each of the elements involved can be provided with its own curve projected into the future. Herein lies the main objection to the method, because the assumption is being made that the elements have no influence on each other. The requirement of numeracy that the inter-relationships be explored is being ignored. The manager using the techniques of statistical projection can be said to be figurate but not yet numerate.

To deal numerately with the problems of prediction it is necessary:

1 to include all the elements in the problem;

2 to establish the relationships that exist between these elements;

3 to deduce conclusions from these relationships by logical rules.

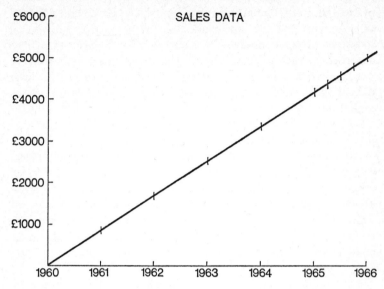

FIG. 12.—Straight line projection of sales data.

An approach which embodies these principles is input-output analysis. Its starting point is the fact that in any industrial system firms sell their products to the consumer and also to each other. First, it is necessary to define the areas of economic operation to be considered. These areas may be as numerous as desired. The limit will normally be set by the limitation of the means available to perform the calculations that ensue. For simplicity, in order to illustrate the methods of input-output analysis, the economic system will be assumed to consist of three areas only:

> manufacturing industry
> commercial services, and
> agricultural industry.

These three areas together with the consumers, both internal operating through home demand, and external operating through the export trade, make up the elements to be analyzed.

Consider the output of manufacturing industry. Some part of this will be absorbed by manufacturing industry itself, retained to help its own production. Of the total output of cars, for instance, some part is required by manufacturing firms to provide official cars for their representatives and senior executives. The remainder of the output of manufacturing industry will be absorbed by the organizations making up commercial services, the agricultural industry and the consumers. The question is, 'How much will be absorbed by each of these areas?' This question can be answered. The answer depends on two things. The first is the general level of economic activity and the second is the stage reached by technological development in the various areas of the system.

Consumer absorption of manufacturing industry is that part of total consumer demand which is used to purchase the products of manufacturing industry. Total consumer demand is largely determined by Government economic policy at any particular time, and, in order to predict the future, assumptions have to be made about what this is likely to be. The proportion of consumer demand which is spent in various areas is known from national statistics and from market research investigations. Assumptions have to be made as to how far ahead these are likely to be valid, or to what extent consumer habits may change.

Agricultural absorption can be calculated if it is known how much of the output of industry is required to produce unit output of agriculture, and what the total output of agriculture is going to be. The amount of industrial output required to produce unit output of agriculture can be defined as the technical co-efficient of agriculture with respect to manufacturing. National statistics will give the deliveries of various manufacturing industries to agriculture and also the total output of agricultural industry. Dividing the former by the latter will give the technical co-efficient of agriculture with respect to manufacturing. An assumption has to be made as to what degree, if at all, technological developments are likely to change this figure for the future. To obtain the agricultural absorption, the technical co-efficient has to be multiplied by the total output of agriculture at the period of time for which the prediction is required. This is one of the items which the prediction is trying to settle, and for the moment it is unknown. It will be found by deduction.

In the same way there can be defined:

1 the technical co-efficient of commercial services with respect to manufacturing; and
2 the technical co-efficient of manufacturing with respect to manufacturing;

which are required for the calculation of services absorption and manufacturing absorption. Again, the total outputs of these items are not known and, like agricultural absorption, will need to be calculated.

All the elements concerning manufacturing industry have now been included and their inter-relationships have been defined. Conclusions from these can be deduced by logical rules, but it is necessary first to translate them into mathematical language.

To do so, let the:

output of services be denoted by S
output of manufacturing industry be denoted by M
output of agriculture be denoted by A
consumer absorption of manufacturing industry be denoted by C_M
technical co-efficient of manufacturing with respect to manufacturing be denoted by T_{MM}
technical co-efficient of services with respect to manufacturing
be denoted by T_{SM}
technical co-efficient of agriculture with respect to manufacturing
be denoted by T_{AM}

Then

manufacturing absorption of manufacturing will be $T_{MM} \times M$
services absorption of manufacturing will be $T_{SM} \times S$
agricultural absorption of manufacturing will be $T_{AM} \times A$.

The statement which has to be translated into mathematical language is that the output of manufacturing is absorbed in the four ways shown. Mathematically this is written

$$M = T_{MM} \times M + T_{SM} \times S + T_{AM} \times A + C_M$$

By following a simple rule of mathematical grammar, this can be rewritten in the form

$$(1 - T_{MM})\ M - T_{SM}\ S - T_{AM}\ A = C_M$$

In the same way, if consumer absorption of services be denoted by C_S, then the

technical co-efficient of manufacturing with respect to services
will be noted by T_{MS}
technical co-efficient of services with respect to services will be
denoted by T_{SS}
technical co-efficient of agriculture with respect to services will
be denoted by T_{AS}

Another statement can be written as follows:

$$-T_{MS}\ M + (1 - T_{SS})\ S - T_{AS}\ A = C_S$$

and also, if consumer absorption of agriculture be denoted by C_A, then the

> technical co-efficient of manufacture with respect to agriculture will be denoted by T_{MA}
> technical co-efficient of services with respect to agriculture will be denoted by T_{SA}
> technical co-efficient of agriculture with respect to agriculture will be denoted by T_{AA}

another statement:

$$-T_{MA}\ M - T_{SA}\ S + (1 - T_{AA})\ A = C_A$$

The task has now become one of drawing conclusions from a situation described mathematically by the three equations. These are as derived above.

$$(1 - T_{MM})\ M - T_{SM}\ S - T_{AM}\ A = C_M$$
$$-T_{MS}\ M + (1 - T_{SS})\ S - T_{AS}\ A = C_S$$
$$-T_{MS}\ M - T_{SS}\ S + (1 - T_{AS})\ A = C_A$$

If the consumer demands for these three areas of the economy are given values, then the situation becomes one where there are three mathematical equations with three unknowns. These can be solved to give values for M, S and A which depend only on the values assumed for consumer demand.

The approach has been illustrated by considering the economy as consisting only of one manufacturing firm, one organization providing services and one agricultural organization. The argument is not affected by breaking each of these down into a number of sub-divisions. Manufacture, for example, can be considered in terms of capital goods, consumer durables and consumer industries, to as fine a degree of detail as desired. Services can be sub-divided into financial, transport, distribution and many other types of services. Agriculture has as its constituent parts dairy products, meat, fruit, vegetables and others. The number of equations to describe the situation must be equal to the number of economic areas to be considered. In the extreme, the economic area may be taken as the individual firm and all other firms whose products it uses and which, in turn, use its own products. The specification of the situation has increased in size but has not changed in character.

What has changed, however, is the nature of the problem facing the manager. He is no longer concerned with developing the solution. The development of the solution is an automatic procedure if the elements of the problem can be correctly identified and measured. The manager need not be concerned with the process of arriving at the implications but needs to concentrate on the correct statement of the problem, the identification of the elements involved and the setting of their measurements. He, in effect, draws up the design of a model, but this time on the conceptual plane and not on the physical plane. He leaves the actual construction and operating of the model to others. This he will normally have been quite prepared to do if the model had been a physical one. He may have some doubts where the model is a conceptual one. It is necessary, nevertheless, that he should leave the mechanics of it to the experts, if the fullest advantage of the techniques available is to be obtained. The danger immediately arises, in consequence, that the manager and the expert will be operating in different worlds. To avoid this danger, numeracy must be called to his aid to provide understanding of what is being attempted and of the validity of the results.

It will be remembered that the distinction was drawn between short-term forecasting and long-term prediction. In the short-term, there is a greater likelihood that the environment to which the forecast is applied can be considered in isolation without loss of accuracy. The interactions between the elements in the environment and elements external to it have less time in which to bring about changes. Moreover, in the short-term, projections of statistical patterns are less likely to go far awry. For short-term forecasting, therefore, the completely numerate approach of model building may use up too much time and resources to be justified. For long-term prediction, elemental forecasting and statistical projection are less reliable methods, because interactions and external influences have more time in which to bring about changes. Control of the situation becomes less, and the need to adopt the numerate approach of creating as complete a conceptual model as possible that much more acute.

The manager's task, though changed, is not diminished or lessened in importance. He it is who must specify, in this instance, which are the organizations whose inter-relationships are to be included, the model and the nature of the inter-relationships, although without defining the mathematical expression of their natures. It is for him, too, to choose the particular values of the consumer demand to be used in working out a solution. He is at liberty to have a number of possibilities examined, and it would then be his task to make the final choice for action.

The process of conceptual model-building is the truly numerate approach to the problems of prediction, and the transformation of the nature of the particular problem facing the manager is typical of the consequences that follow the adoption of any numerate approach.

PROBLEMS OF ANALYSIS

Prediction identifies the design of the backcloth against which the affairs of the organization are to be conducted. Both the strategy and the tactics to be employed in conducting affairs now have to be worked out. To do this successfully involves analysing the situations in their various aspects. Some of the tools of numeracy that are available to the manager in this task have been discussed in the previous chapter and examples given of subdivisions of this major category. These can be referred to as problems of analysis. It is in this area where most of the advance has been made in using numerate techniques for decision-making.

As always, when the approach becomes numerate the particular tasks facing the manager do not lie in the actual process of arriving at the decision, but in specifying in some detail the problem to be solved and in knowing whether a numerate approach is appropriate or not.

The manager must, first, be able to identify the problem facing him, so that it can be pigeon-holed. This requires him to look at it in terms of its fundamental nature as a problem of conflict or an allocation problem or a waiting time problem and so on, rather than in terms of its application as a sales problem or a production problem or a finance problem, for example. Alternatively, he must be in a position to know that the problem he is tackling is not one for which numerate techniques exist.

The manager must, secondly, specify all the elements that are to be taken into consideration. There is a cautionary tale concerning the long-service employee of an organization which gave gold watches to its staff on the completion of every twenty-five years' service. This staff member had acquired two watches, the first after twenty-five years' service and the second after fifty years' service. One day later he retired and was faced with the need to cut his coat according to the cloth of a pension much less than his previous salary. His wife insisted, therefore, on one of the gold watches being sold, but the question was which one. The earlier of the two watches had long since ceased to go. The second had been checked against a time signal and found to be losing three seconds every twenty-four hours. His wife had no doubts as to which watch should be sold, but her husband determined to put the problem on to his old firm's computer. He knew that a programme existed which would examine alternatives to identify, in this case, which watch told the right time most often. From the computer he received the answer: 'Keep the watch you got twenty-five years ago and sell the one you got yesterday.' His wife considered it ridiculous to retain a watch which no longer went but agreed to delay action until an explanation of the decision could be obtained from the computer. This, when it was received, stated: 'The watch which you got twenty-five years ago tells the right time twice every twenty-four hours, but the watch which you got yesterday tells the right time only once every twenty-eight years.' This is the devastatingly logical answer to the problem as stated.

If one of the elements to it is that only watches which are going are to be considered, then this needs stating. This is so whether one is using a computer or not, if logical automatic problem-solving procedures are to be adopted. The responsibility for stating the conditions is one which the manager must assume. In the much more flexible decision-making processes of the past, no manager existed who was not rescued at some time or another by his staff, who knew that he had omitted some essential part in his statement of the problem they were working on and acted accordingly. The more complex the problems of today become and the more automatic the techniques used, the more inflexible does the decision-making process become and the greater the importance to be attached to the statement of the problem. Succour becomes less and less available.

The numerate manager, too, must be aware of the considerations that apply to the choice of the units of measurement. It has long been customary to express the elements of a problem in financial terms, and a monetary unit of measurement has the considerable merit of providing a common yardstick for elements which have a variety of characteristics. Except when one is dealing only with cash flows, however, it has the disadvantage of being a derived unit. That is, it is formed by multiplying the natural unit of the element being measured and a 'price' per unit. Deductions from problems expressed in financial terms therefore always reflect movements in both these units taken together and never in one or the other separately. This disadvantage is tacitly recognized by economists and others whenever problems are worked through in 'real terms' or when prices are adjusted by an index referred to a particular year as a base. To adjust the financial unit of measurement in this way is often an unnecessary complication adding to the work involved. This can be avoided by stating, wherever possible, the elements in their natural unit of measurement. This is not to say that finance is to be ignored in problem-solving, but it is to be considered as only one of the elements in a situation.

Two examples will illustrate the point. If the critical factor for a particular decision is the possibility of obtaining or not obtaining the necessary numbers of work people, then to measure the factor in terms of cost is obscuring rather than enlightening. Then, again, the future operations of a computer manufacturing company are dependent on the actual numbers and types of the computers that are being delivered or on order. These determine the degree of maintenance and other supporting services that are going to be necessary, the work load that is going to be put on to the factory and the probability of replacement or expansion orders in the future. The bald information that the order book has increased by £5 million is of little help for the necessary decision-making processes in this case.

It must not be supposed that the units of measurement are necessarily numerical. To assign an order of preference, to equate the action taken on marketing a product with its characteristics, to compare in qualitative descriptive terms the results of different decisions, are all expressions in the field of numeracy. 'Order of preference,' 'equate,' 'compare,' are numerate terms. To employ logical deduction to arrive at a solution is to use a numerate technique.

The following problem is one to be tackled by organization of knowledge, measurement and the use of logic, which are the attributes of numeracy. The unit of measurement here is *compatibility of proposals with facts and opinions*.

A firm is about to launch five new products, *A*, *B*, *C*, *D* and *E*, which are defined in price ranges, though not necessarily in that order, as

> luxury
> expensive
> moderate
> normal
> inexpensive

The products are to be coloured, each in a different colour

> red
> blue
> green
> yellow
> black

The products are designed for the female population, which is divided into the following classes:

> middle class
> lower class
> housewives
> older women
> teenage girls

No person is to be considered as belonging to more than one class. The choices of advertising media open are

> hoardings
> daily newspapers
> weekly periodicals
> cinema
> television

Five amounts of advertising appropriation are laid down

> £20,000
> £15,000
> £10,000
> £5,000
> £3,000

One, and only one, of these appropriations is to be allotted to each medium.

The following pieces of information available, or opinions held, are to be the basis of the marketing decisions:

1 product A is to be red
2 product D is to be given £5,000 advertising appropriation
3 housewives prefer green as a colour
4 product E appeals to the middle class
5 the product coloured green must be in the price range immediately below the product coloured black
6 television advertising is to have £10,000 allotted to it
7 the product coloured yellow is to be advertised on hoardings
8 teenage girls buy products in the moderate price range
9 product C is to be the luxury class product
10 cinema advertising is to have the next highest appropriation after that allocated to hoardings
11 hoardings are to be used to advertise the product whose price range is either immediately above or below the product to which is allocated £15,000
12 the advertising medium most likely to reach the lower class is the daily newspaper
13 weekly periodicals are to be used to advertise the inexpensive product
14 The expensive product is to be coloured blue.

No other information is available and no other opinions are held sufficiently strongly to affect decisions concerning the marketing plan.

It is an exercise requiring numeracy to provide a plan which will conform to the information known and opinions held, and which will show the products in their price ranges, the colour to be used for each, the class of the population to which each is to be directed, and the form and appropriation of the advertising.

Organization of knowledge is the first mark of the numerate approach and to solve this problem a framework should be drawn up, into which final assignments can be put as they are ascertained.

Price Range	Luxury	Expensive	Moderate	Normal	Inexpensive
Product					
Colour					
Customer class					
Advertising medium					
Appropriation					

To provide a starting point, the price ranges can be inserted in descending order.

A study of the pieces of information given will reveal that certain of them permit no latitude at all in some assignments. Thus, (9) defines product *C* as luxury, (14) defines the expensive product as blue and (13) defines the advertising medium of the inexpensive product as weekly periodicals, while (8) nominates the class of customer for the moderately priced product.

Price Range	Luxury	Expensive	Moderate	Normal	Inexpensive
Product	C				
Colour		blue			
Customer class			teenage girls		
Advertising medium					weekly periodicals
Appropriation					

(1) and (5) taken together, and with decisions already made, mean that colours red, green and black must be reserved for the moderate, normal and inexpensive products, but as yet it cannot be definitely stated which. This in turn, however, means that the luxury product must be yellow and (7) that the advertising medium for that product must be hoardings, while (11) requires that the appropriation for the expensive product must be £15,000. The situation becomes, either

Price Range	Luxury	Expensive	Moderate	Normal	Inexpensive
Product	C		A		
Colour	yellow	blue	red	black	green
Customer class			teenage girls		
Advertising medium	hoardings				weekly periodicals
Appropriation		£15,000			

or

Price Range	Luxury	Expensive	Moderate	Normal	Inexpensive
Product	C				A
Colour	yellow	blue	black	green	red
Customer class			teenage girls		
Advertising medium	hoardings				weekly periodicals
Appropriation		£15,000			

From now on, alternatives have to be considered, discarding those which lead to a situation in which some of the conditions cannot be fulfilled. Ultimately a solution which is compatible with all the conditions will emerge. Readers may like to find this and compare theirs with the solution derived in the appendix.

This example is really the carrying out of a feasibility study and this, and all the problems so far considered under this heading in the previous chapter on problems of analysis, can be tackled by numerate methods. Two of the problems which arise, however, after the analysis has been performed are only in part amenable to numeracy. First is the assessment of the degree of the accuracy of the solution resulting from the analysis. Numerate techniques derived from the theory of errors and statistical theory will define a measure of the accuracy of the solution, but in the event that this is not sufficient, recourse must be had to non-numerate methods. Supporting evidence may be obtainable from a study of practices similar to the one for which a solution is being sought. On its own this would be a dangerous course to follow, since the elements in the two situations might not be exactly similar, but taken in conjunction with more soundly based conclusions it can be legitimately envisaged. A consideration of the experience of competitors in a field similar to that which one is contemplating entering can be used to confirm or throw doubts on, but never refute one's own conclusions. In the last resort, a physical pilot study may need to be organized in an attempt to provide auxiliary evidence to that already deduced from the conceptual model.

The other problem which should not be ignored is to deduce what effect the action taken following the solution will have on the elements of the problem itself. An example of this is the so-called 'band wagon' effect of political public opinion polls at election times. It is surmised that results published in a poll of an advantage held by one party or another result in many of those who had indicated to the pollster their intention of voting for the opposing party switching their allegiance. The result is to give to a trend, which at the time of measurement was correctly identified, a more powerful movement than predicted. Whether this be so or not in the political case, the likely influence of the actions taken on the elements of the situation from which the solution was derived *must* be considered. They must be taken into account when the outcome of the action is being measured. The action not yet having taken place, knowledge concerning its possible relationships with the elements under consideration will be scanty. These relationships are not the same thing as the relationships between the elements, from which the action which is to be taken is deduced. Nevertheless, allowances must be made for them.

PROBLEMS OF LEADERSHIP

Decisions reached after expert analysis and against a backcloth accurately predicted still need to be implemented. It is not the intention, here, to investigate the question whether a good decision badly implemented is better than a bad decision well implemented. *Both* the process of decision-making and the implementation of the decisions are *necessary* functions of management. The latter function will require at some stage to operate through men and women. This constitutes the leadership function.

What constitutes leadership is a question to which there is no single or definite answer. The writers and speakers on the subject propound very varying views. It is almost a question of '*quot homines, tot sententiae.*' Amongst the many differences of view, however, a few commonly held opinions can be discerned.

The first is the need for self-education. Admiral Sir Denis Boyd, in his Maclaren Memorial Lecture in 1953, put it this way: 'A great leader would be the first to agree that no-one can teach you to lead: nor do I think it is a subject you can learn. The art of leadership is not a thing you receive from outside, but springs from your own heart and your energy.' Captain S. W. Roskill, R.N., in his book *The Art of Leadership* put it rather more strongly. He wrote: 'What is certain is that today the educational requirements demanded of the leader are heavier than before,' and again 'It is my belief that the degree of success which he achieves in the later phases of his career, when human interests are replacing the technical demands of the early years, depends chiefly on his perseverance in self-education. And the field of study from which he will be able to reap the harvest of wisdom and understanding then needed is that broadly known as the "humanities." Hence arises the need for the leader to read constantly and widely—perhaps especially in the field of past and recent history.' Professor Macrae, now Principal of Ashridge Management College, in a lecture delivered in 1958 in Glasgow, talked about 'Leadership in Industry' and had this to say: 'A little learning is proverbially a dangerous thing and in the spread of imperfect knowledge lies the gravest danger of disaster to our civilization, as disaster has come before to earlier civilizations from this cause. The only way to salvation, as I see it, is to spread fuller and better knowledge before the imperfect has time to erupt in irreparable destruction. So far from being the Cinderella in practical value, as it has too often been regarded, education is the need and the hope transcending all else. By improving education and by laying its benefits within the reach of all, not only will the qualities that make for leadership be stimulated and fostered throughout the population, but the pre-eminent in these qualities and aptitudes will be readily identifiable.'

These extracts show unanimity in recognizing the value of knowledge in the practice of leadership and of the need for the leader to be educated. The question for discussion in the context of this book is how far *numerate* knowledge is a necessary attribute for the exercise of his function of leadership.

The distinction is here drawn between the manager's function of decision-making and his function of leadership. A leader, of course, also has decisions to make but these are of a tactical nature. They often arise when something has gone wrong or some unforeseen circumstance has arisen. Usually time in which to arrive at a decision is limited and the opportunities to examine every circumstance not presented. While alertness in recognizing situations and intelligence in relating them to past experience will always be attributes necessary for the formulation of such decisions, there can be little scope for employing numeracy to take the broad view, define and measure all the elements, examine their inter-relationships and apply the tools of logic in arriving at the decision.

The principal elements in leadership situations are human beings. Immediately problems arise in devising accurate means of measurement. Social scientists can offer help, but their science is a very young one, has not yet identified all the elements for study and has neither defined the inter-relationships existing nor provided sufficiently accurate measuring devices for quantitative decision-making. M. Maurice Duverger in his *Introduction to the Social Sciences*, as translated by Malcolm Anderson of Manchester University, is quite frank about it. 'The relative positions of theory and practice differ between the social and the physical sciences. In the physical sciences progress in theory precedes practical application; the reverse is the case in the social sciences where practice seems more advanced than theory. There is a striking contrast between the effectiveness of the applied social sciences and the anarchic state of their theory: sociologists are not even agreed on elementary definitions and basic concepts. Each sociologist talks his own language and this makes communication between sociologists difficult.'

As yet, therefore, although figurate techniques can certainly be used, it is too early for numeracy to be a required quality for a leader practising the precepts of social science.

There is a sense, indeed, in which numeracy may be the enemy of good leadership. The leader must avoid any appearance of vacillation. To lead successfully he must exude confidence. A decision once made should not have doubts cast upon it once action has started, and the leader's function is not to reconsider decisions. A phrase often quoted in management discussions is: 'I have made up my mind, don't confuse me with the facts.' This has been criticized in some quarters as not being in keeping with modern management methods. It is true that, while the process of decision-making is in progress, facts must always be out in the open and never ignored. By contrast, once the decision has been taken and the action planned, time spent by the leader during action in considering facts may be time wasted. There are other means of controlling progress which can be employed.

Leaders, of course, have a part to play in the process of arriving at decisions. In this context they rank as experts with advice to give on the expected behaviour of the elements they themselves control. This advice is localized and draws on a knowledge in depth and on experience of the effect of actual or proposed courses of action on their own situations. However, it is uni-directional and is not concerned with how the reactions from their own spheres of influence will affect other elements nor with an assessment of the relative importances of the actions and reactions. It is therefore not a numerate approach.

PROBLEMS OF ORGANIZATION

There are always two major tasks for any enterprise. These are, first, to discover what should be done and, secondly, to do it. To complete either task successfully requires organization. Problems of organization occur in both.

The organization set up to implement decision is primarily a framework in which leadership can operate. The types of problems which arise directly in the exercise of the leadership function have

H

already been considered. In addition to them other problems arise when considering the organization itself. These are concerned with communication, motivation and the whole field of human and industrial relations. The solutions to them determine the organizational structure and the operating procedures. To these further problems the same arguments apply as to the problems which originate directly from the functioning of leadership. As yet, the numerate approach is of little help, and numeracy is not required for the manager concerned with them.

It does not follow that the same is true for organization problems arising from decision-making. The pyramidal organization structure for an enterprise is of honourable ancestry. From the time of Henri Fayol, its first publicist, the implications of this structure, its ramifications and the foundations and struts necessary to support and strengthen it have been intensively studied. The conclusions of these studies have been widely approved and applied.

The objects of these studies have been to provide operating rules for enterprises to achieve success against some particular backcloth of circumstance and environment. The problems of designing and constructing the backcloth, it has largely been assumed, could be handled by the same organization in much the same sort of way. More recently, some consideration has been given to the processes of decision-making both in theory and in practice. The solutions propounded to the problems arising have largely been along the lines of grafting committee systems to the existing structure.

The committees have not often been considered in any other light than as a service to the parts of the organization structure. Attitudes to them have been uneasy and ill-defined. Admiral Boyd, in the lecture on leadership previously mentioned, says of his war-time Commander-in-Chief 'his direct uncompromising hostility to all he considered evil was his great characteristic. One thing, I think, above all others annoyed him, and that was the evil of executive committees,' and again later: 'Call committees to study, report and advise, but the action must be human. . . .' This would not be an untypical view taken by those executives responsible for action and the omission of the word 'decide' from the roles to be played by a committee would be regarded as fitting. Herein lies the fundamental problem in organizing for decision-making. In which quarter should lie the responsibility for the actual taking of the decision?

It needs to be noticed that there is a basic difference between the starting point for the decision-making process and the starting point for exercising the leadership function in action. In decision-making the assumption is that the truth is not yet known and that neither is it known in advance *where* the truth lies. The task of the decision-maker is to uncover *all* the sources of truth and to combine what is revealed there into a decision. In contrast, the assumption in leadership is that the truth is known. The task of the leader is to translate the truth into action and to control the action. Numeracy, it has been seen, does not help in this latter task. How far can it help in settling the best form of organization for decision-making?

Information theory throws some light on this type of problem. Consider two channels of information conveying to a decision-making area one each of two separate pieces of information. The decision to be made is based on these two pieces of information and on nothing else. It is necessary to assess the efficiency of each of the communication channels and of the decision-making area. One way of expressing these efficiencies is to estimate the probability of each communication channel correctly transmitting the information and of the correct decision being made in the decision-making area. Suppose these probabilities are 0·7 (70%) for each communication channel and 0·8 (80%) for the decision-making process. Then the probability of the decision being correct is $0·7 \times 0·7 \times 0·8$, or 0·392 (i.e., 39·2%). If the information and the decision can be regarded in these black and white terms as either wholly right or wholly wrong, this means that fewer than forty decisions in every hundred will be correct. Now this description is representative of the situation where a decision is taken by a single executive receiving advice independently from two separate advisers. What the levels of efficiency of the channels of communication and of the decision-making area are likely to be in any particular case are matters of opinion. Opinions that have been expressed on the 70 per cent and 80 per cent levels chosen for this example are that these are not too low for the majority of enterprises. The probability of arriving at correct decisions in such a system is not high. To improve its efficiency without changing the type of system requires that the efficiencies be raised to the highest possible level.

It will be observed that the efficiency of the final decision is largely governed by the efficiencies of the individual channels of communication in transmitting true facts. This applies not only to the physical transmission of information through communications systems but also to the making apparent of truths by argument in decision-making areas. If these channels, both in the physical and the mental sense, are single channels for each element of information, then it is very difficult to improve the efficiency of the final decision. To improve the individual channels in the physical case involves expenditure, which after a certain level of efficiency has been reached may be quite large. In the mental sense improvement of efficiency depends on how far it is possible for one mind to encompass all the facts of a particular area of information. Again, beyond a certain level of efficiency this is very difficult to achieve, and a 90 per cent efficiency is normally regarded as very high. With a 90 per cent level of communication in the example previously considered, the efficiency of the final decision becomes $90\% \times 90\%$ $\times 80\%$, or $64 \cdot 8\%$. If the decision is to take into account three areas of information, then the efficiency of the final decision is $90\% \times 90\% \times 90\% \times 80\%$, or $58 \cdot 32\%$. Thus, in this type of decision-making system, a quite large effort in improving the efficiency of each of two channels of information still leaves more than 30 out of every 100 of the decisions as wrong. To push the efficiency of the decision any higher would involve an expenditure of money or time or mental effort which most people would regard as inordinate. Information theory does, however, indicate a reasonable method by which the efficiency of the final decision can be increased. One finds that by increasing the number of channels along which any piece of information flows the probability of the decision-making process being applied to correct information rather than incorrect information goes up markedly. This, of course, is merely the theoretical justification expressed in mathematical form for the ordinary commercial practice of, for example, sending confirmatory copies by mail of messages transmitted by cable. The additional channels need not be as different in method as mail and cable. They may indeed be identical but operating at different times or by different routes. What is important is that the number of channels needed to attain any given required probability of correct receipt of information is capable of being calculated. What is of further importance is that the same argument is valid in the making known of truths on the mental plane.

This is the justification for the committee system as a method of *reaching* decisions as distinct from *implementing* them. If the capacities of different individuals in an organization for possessing correct information on one subject or another can be estimated, then a numerate method can be used to decide on the membership of any particular committee. This will require the defining of a particular probability of reaching decisions which will be acceptable. 100 per cent probability, i.e. certainty, cannot be achieved, but the probabilities that can be reached by varying combinations of members of the organization can be calculated and compared with the target.

There are other supporting reasons for a committee system of decision-making. These are not numerate but are closely related to numeracy. The purpose of numeracy is to arrive at an objective assessment of the truth. The committee system helps to foster this purpose. One of the problems of arriving at the truth is the fact that those who possess the truth in greatest measure are not always those who are most efficient in expressing it. The alliance and publicity of a committee can give strength to one who in a private *tête-à-tête* consultation may be tongue-tied or overpowered by the personalities of others. Much depends, here, on the choice of chairman, but irrespective of the chairman a committee, judiciously chosen, can gather a momentum of its own. The objective of any decision-making process is to make the facts speak for themselves, and a further advantage of using a committee is that, if the objective is achieved, the conclusions are seen publicly to be inevitable.

The decision-making process is not complete until all the considerations that affect the implementation of a decision are known. This is the planning stage. Mankind has made attempts to plan his activities from the earliest days. Gradually his methods of planning have developed and expanded. In recent years these have culminated in a group of planning techniques whose generic title is critical path, and which exemplify numeracy in action. In particular, critical path techniques are solidly based on:

1 a broad comprehensive approach to a problem or decision;
2 a definition of the interrelationship of different parts of a problem or decision;
3 the measurement of all the elements in a problem or decision;
4 the application of logical deductive methods to the elements in order to arrive at conclusions;
5 the courage to accept the conclusions.

The basis of the approach can be understood from the following example of a plan to prepare a computer programme. For a fuller understanding of the techniques of critical path, reference should be made to one or more of the books listed in the bibliography on pp. 217-218.

The operation must start with the preparation of a feasibility study from which will be determined two things:

1 the nature and type of the computing system to be ordered;
2 the operating system which is to be followed when the computer is used.

A Stonehenge type decision-maker would concentrate on the planning of the second of these operations and would, in that context, quite correctly distinguish the following stages:

(5.0) 1 preparation of systems analysis;
(15.0) 2 preparation of systems flow charts;
(5.0) 3 writing of computer programmes;
(3.0) 4 preparation of data for testing programmes;
(5.0) 5 testing the programmes;
(3.0) 6 correction of programmes.

He would rely on others to do the planning for the following actions:

1 preparation of computer order, progressing of delivery and carrying out acceptance tests;
2 training of programmers and making them familiar with flow charts;
3 training of computer operators and making them familiar with programmes, operators here being taken to include those who will prepare input materials;
4 preparation of site for the computer and arranging auxiliary equipment.

These separate plans, coupled with estimates of how long each stage will take, can be brought together and presented in the form of a bar chart. Such bar charts as, for example, Gantt charts, have long been used for showing sequences of operations in production scheduling. Figure 13 shows the five separate sequences of operations listed above, with the times for each stage represented by the length of the appropriate section of each bar. All the times are measured in weeks and are shown in figures in each section.

A bar chart of this type will show quite clearly the variation in time required for each stage of the whole project, and also which

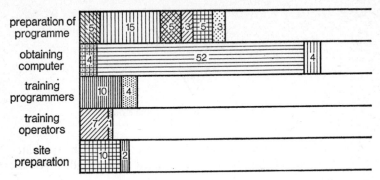

FIG. 13.—A bar chart for computer installation planning.

of the subdivisions of the project is going to take the longest time.
In this case it is the task of obtaining the computer.

However, there are a number of questions for which the bar
chart cannot supply the answers. These are:

1 how long after the project starts will it be before the programme
   is ready?
2 when can work on each of the stages start?
3 which parts of the project need the closest control?

It is in order to provide the answers to such questions that
critical path is used and it requires on the part both of its practitioners, and also of the managers making use of it, an expansion
of the figurate approach, which is sufficient for the preparation of
bar charts, to a numerate approach.

First, it is necessary to identify the really fundamental activities
in the project. Thus, for instance, the stage listed as 'preparation of
systems analysis' needs to be broken down further because there
are two distinct activities involved. One of these, the general part
which would apply no matter what type of computer system was
to be installed, can proceed without waiting to discover the specification of the computer system. The other part, however, is specific
to the particular computer system which is ordered, and therefore
cannot commence until the computer order is placed. These
fundamental elements in the project can be shown visually in an
arrow diagram, in which the stages of the project are shown as
triangles and the activity involved in getting from one stage to
another as arrows, with the arrowheads showing the direction of
progress (see Figure 14).

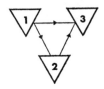

FIG. 14.—Arrow diagram—stage one.

The stages or milestones in the project are known as events, and in the part of the project just depicted they are identified as:

Event	Description
1	Start of project
2	Computer order placed
3	Systems analysis completed

Here it is assumed that the feasibility study has already been carried out and that the placing of the computer order involves only settling the details of the system to be obtained. The activities of this part of the project can also be described and are defined by the events at the start and finish of the activity.

Activities	Description
1–2	Preparing computer order
1–3	Doing general systems analysis
2–3	Doing specific systems analysis

Continuing in this way one can compile a complete list of the events in the project.

Event	Description
1	Start of project
2	Computer order placed
3	Systems analysis completed
4	Systems flow charts completed
5	Programmers trained
6	Computer operators trained
7	Site prepared
8	Computer delivered
9	Programmes written
10	Test data prepared
11	Programme test begun
12	Programme test completed
13	Programme corrected

It is now necessary to consider very carefully how these events relate to each other and what are the activities that both lead to each event and follow from it. For example, once event 2, computer order placed, is reached, a number of things can follow. These are:

1 the training of the programmers leading to event 5;
2 the training of the computer operators leading to event 6;
3 the preparation of the site leading to event 7;
4 the progressing of the delivery of the computer leading to event 8.

The arrow diagram can now be extended, as in Figure 15.

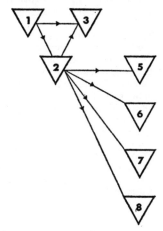

FIG. 15.—Arrow diagram—stage two.

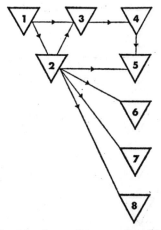

FIG. 16.—Arrow diagram—stage three.

However, the programmers will not be fully trained for this project until they have understood the flow charts. These will have been prepared while the training of the programmers was going on, but a start to their preparation would have to wait until the systems analysis was complete. These relationships can now be added to the arrow diagram (see Figure 16).

The complete list of the activities identified in this way is:

Activities	Description
1–2	Preparing computer order
1–3	Doing general systems analysis
2–3	Doing specific systems analysis
2–5	Training programmers
2–6	Training computer operators
2–7	Preparing site for computer
2–8	Progressing delivery of computer
3–4	Drawing systems flow charts
4–5	Familiarizing programmers with flow charts
5–9	Writing of programmes
6–11	Operator's preparation for programme testing
7–11	Assembling of auxiliary equipment for test
8–11	Carrying out acceptance tests on computer
9–6	Familiarizing operators with programmes
9–10	Preparing test data
10–11	Making test data available for programme test
11–12	Carrying out testing of programme
12–13	Correcting errors in programme

The inter-relationships of events and activities is shown in the complete arrow diagram of Figure 17.

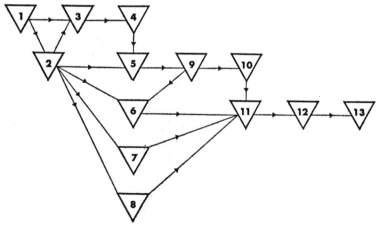

FIG. 17.—Arrow diagram—stage four.

This should be compared with the bar chart presentation of the planning of the same project. It will be observed that the logic of the complete project has been depicted in the arrow diagram, in contrast to the separate logics of the separate parts of the project in the bar chart. The bar chart, however, did successfully represent the times of the activities, and this is as yet lacking in the arrow diagram.

These times must be obtained by whatever means are best suited, as they must in any other method of planning. This may be by using quoted delivery times if considered reliable, or adjusted if not. It may be by using work study technique to measure activities or it may be by using experience to provide estimates. Whatever the methods used, the times must be accepted by the decision-makers since these times, together with the logical analysis of the activities represented by the arrow diagram, are the basis of the deductions that follow. The times are incorporated in the diagram by writing them alongside the arrows to which they refer (Figure 18).

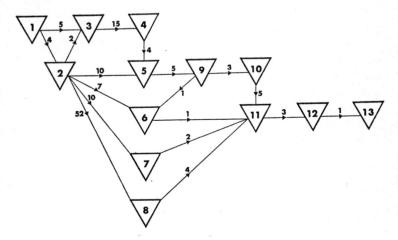

FIG. 18.—Arrow diagram showing time measurements.

As numeracy requires, the project has now been viewed as a whole, its elements have been identified and their inter-relationships defined, and measurements have been incorporated. It remains to harness the power of logic. In critical path the logic is straightforward and no sophisticated mathematics is necessary.

The starting point of the project is taken as zero and the argument runs as follows.

If zero is the starting point for event 1, and if it takes four weeks to complete the activity 1–2, then four weeks after the start of the project is the earliest time that the stage represented by event 2 can be reached. This is shown in Figure 19.

FIG. 19.—Arrow diagram with earliest event times—stage one.

Now consider event 3. There are two separate activities that must be completed before the stage of the project represented by event 3 is reached.

The activity 1–3 which is the general systems analysis can be completed by $0+5 = 5$ weeks after the start of the project. The other activity leading to event 3 is 2–3, which represents the specific systems analysis, and this takes 2 weeks. It cannot start until the computer order is placed and the earliest time for this has been found to be 4. So the earliest time for completing the activity 2–3 is $4+2 = 6$ weeks after the start of the project. Event 3 is dependent on activity 1–3, earliest time 5, and on activity 2–3, earliest time 6. Both must be allowed for, and so the latest of these 2 times must be taken for event 3 (see Figure 20).

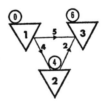

FIG. 20.—Arrow diagram with earliest event times—stage two.

Earliest possible times of completion can be calculated in this fashion for every stage of the project. The arrow diagram now becomes as shown in Figure 21.

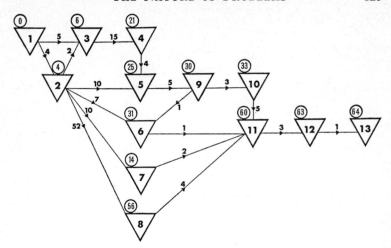

FIG. 21.—Arrow diagram complete with earliest event times.

This establishes a timing sequence for the project and, in particular, it reveals what is the earliest completion date for the project. If none of the conditions specified for the project can be altered, then this final completion date is also unalterable. But if this earliest completion date does have to be accepted without option, it is open to the manager to lay down that it is also the latest date that he will tolerate. Working backwards through the project, latest finishing dates for each stage of the project can then be calculated and inserted below the symbol for each event.

Thus, for instance, for event 12 the latest finishing date that can be tolerated is week 63, since one week must be allowed for the activity 12–13, and week 64 is the latest date that can be tolerated for event 13. In a similar way, week 60 is found to be the latest finishing date for event 11 (see Figure 22).

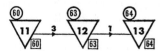

FIG. 22.—Arrow diagram with latest event times—stage one.

Subtracting activity durations in this way, the final arrow diagram becomes as shown in Figure 23.

In calculating these latest finishing times, care has to be taken to allow for all the activities that emerge from each event and to

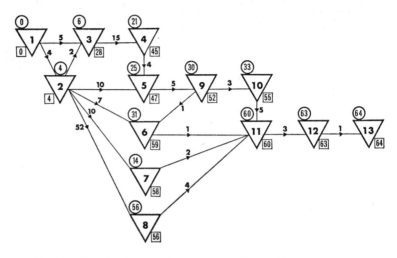

FIG. 23.—Completed arrow diagram with earliest and latest event times.

fix a time which is early enough to permit each of them to be completed. Consider, for example, event 9. Two activities follow from this event, 9–6 and 9–10.

The duration of 9–6 is 1, the latest time for event 6 is week 59, and so a latest time of week 58 would be permissible for event 9 if 9–6 were the only activity to be considered. However, there is also 9–10 to be considered. The duration of this activity is 3. A latest time of week 58 for event 9 would mean that event 10 would not be reached until week 61, whereas week 55 is the latest time that can be tolerated. A little thought will show that to allow both these activities to be completed before the latest finishing times of the events they lead to requires week 52 to be the latest time for event 9.

If the arrow diagram is now studied, it will be seen that for some events the earliest times and the latest times are different, while for other events they are the same. In the form of the arrow diagram drawn here the name *slack* is given to the difference between the earliest and the latest times. Those events where this difference is zero are said to have zero slack.

A path can be drawn through any network connecting those events which have zero slack. This is the *critical path* for the project. In this example, the critical path runs 1–2–8–11–12–13. For the events along this path the earliest times that can occur are the same as the latest times that can be tolerated. There is no slack to be taken up. Every activity along the path is critical and must be rigidly controlled.

The final date for the project is determined by the duration of the activities on the critical path, and if an improvement in the final date is desired it can only be achieved by shortening, in the first instance, the time taken by those activities. This may be achieved by working overtime on some of them. The possible improvement in the final date can be estimated and the cost of achieving it can be calculated. It will be seen that blanket instructions to all departments to work overtime to effect an improvement is to incur unnecessary cost. Up to the amount of slack that is available for each section of the project no improvement is possible.

The amount of slack that is available is a measure of the under-employment of resources. From the information obtained by drawing networks of this type, the scheduling of resources can be improved. Moreover, guidance can be sought from them as to the effect of alterations in plans due to hold-ups. If the delays are shorter than the slack available, no harm will be done to the final completion date. If they are greater, then the network can be redrawn to calculate the effect.

There is much more to be said regarding the use of critical path techniques. Some suggested further reading is contained in the bibliography on pp. 217-218. For use in solving problems of organization, critical path techniques are extremely valuable, are becoming widely used and are numerate.

PROBLEMS OF ATTITUDE

Anyone exercising a managerial function is faced with a decision as to the attitude he should adopt towards his tasks. The problems he encounters in coming to that decision are really the fundamental problems of management.

Examples of the questions for which the manager must find his own answers are:

1 Is the aim of the enterprise to be as efficient as possible at all times or is it merely to achieve some pre-determined target? These are two different aims. The latter aim is simpler, and for it the familiar control procedures of standard costing and budgetary control will in general suffice. The former is much

harder, and poses the problem of defining efficiency and discovering methods by which maximum efficiency can be achieved and maintained through changing circumstances.

2 What is the motivating power which should govern the choice of the unit of measurement for efficiency? Profit? Growth? Security of employment?

3 What restraints on action are recognized, other than the law? Ethics, Christian or other? Public opinion? The desire for a quiet life?

These questions are moral or philosophical questions and neither numeracy, literacy, energy, alertness or intelligence helps to find the answers. The answers come from the faiths and beliefs of those involved. What the answers are determine very largely the direction in which progress in management is made in the future.

Whatever the answers, an understanding of the nature of the problems that are encountered in management is necessary. The analysis has shown that these problems are of two broad classes —those where numerate methods are necessary and those where numeracy is not appropriate. The function of management is exercised at all levels of authority in a number of decision-making areas. In those areas where the problems must be tackled by non-numerate methods, the subjective influences are the most powerful. These areas may without harm be embedded in the traditional structure of line management. In other areas, where numerate methods are appropriate, success is only achieved when complete and objective truth is unambiguously revealed. The subjective influences of personality and authority may prevent this. Other forms of structure than conventional line management need to be devised. The manager himself may be one of the decision-making areas, but he needs to be involved in all of them though not necessarily controlling them. His exercise of control may prevent an objective approach to the problem. This poses a dilemma for the manager as presently conceived, and its resolution may also require a new form of managerial structure. This question will be examined in the chapter 'Manager at the Cross Roads.'

CHAPTER IV

HANDLING INFORMATION

A PARALLEL can be drawn between the process of decision-making and manufacturing. The end product of the former is the action taken as a result of the decision, while the decision itself can be thought of as work-in-progress. Just as work-in-progress comes into being only to be turned into a finished product, so decisions are made only for action to follow. The techniques employed in arriving at the decisions are analogous to the manufacturing processes. Finally, the raw material from which the end product is fashioned is the information which is available to the decision-maker.

The manufacturer of a physical product may have available to him a wide range of raw materials. From these he selects what is appropriate for his needs. Similarly, the decision-maker has a mass of data from which he must extract what is relevant to his purpose. This extracted data is *information*, the raw material for his processes. Data is first condensed into information, and from this information *meaning* is distilled. These are the information handling operations in decision-making. The numerate manager must acquaint himself with the properties of the different sorts of material that he is handling, and acquire a knowledge of the fundamentals of the processes of condensing information and distilling meaning. The techniques of the distillation process have already been dealt with. In this chapter matters relating to the condensing process will be considered.

The Stonehenge type of decision-making examined in the first chapter required no equipment whatsoever. It was the equivalent of a manual system with the data-information-meaning sequence occurring in the mind of the chief. Only the final decision was revealed. This form of decision-making is still appropriate for certain purposes, mainly tactical, in the field of leadership. It is not in practice, of course, entirely absent in strategic decision-making as carried out by strong characters with autocractic inclinations. Its appropriateness then needs to be questioned.

I

Such operations did not continue for long to be performed solely on the mental plane. Forms of recording data and information, and equipment to help in distilling meaning, soon came on the scene. Rudimentary at first, in the shape of notches on tally-sticks and abacus frames, they had steadily become more sophisticated, more varied and more efficient. The culmination, as of today, is the *automatic electronic digital computing system*. Each of these last five words is of significance, and each is essential to a description of what has come to be the symbol of the present age.

AUTOMATIC ELECTRONIC DIGITAL COMPUTING SYSTEMS

The last of the five words is system. Part of the system is a computer and the title 'computer' is often taken as synonymous with the whole. Its use, however, obscures the fact that, on its own, a computer achieves nothing. It has to be provided with auxiliaries. Some of these are human—programmers, systems analysts, punch operators and the like. Others consist of different types of equipment —printers, data links, tape-editing equipment and the like, not to speak of filing cabinets, cupboards and other familiar pieces of office furniture. The auxiliaries are the interface between the computer and the administrative system which forms the environment in which and for which the computer is used. The auxiliaries and the computer make up the computing system. As much care is needed in choosing the auxiliaries as in choosing the computer itself. Poor choices of these will result not only in the operations of the computer being performed less efficiently than they might be, but also in a failure to integrate successfully the two systems, administrative and computing. Less than efficient working of a computer occurs, for example, if the speed at which a printer can accept the signals is less than the speed at which the computer can provide them. Friction between the two systems may occur if those responsible for analysing the system of any task proposed for computer working fail to understand the essential needs of the administrative system.

It is a computing system. The word 'computing' however is not to be thought of merely in the narrow sense of 'performing numerical calculations'. Much of the work of a computing system is, of course, doing just that, but to confine a computer to doing numerical calculations in the normal sense of those words is to fail to realize its potentialities fully. Computing comprises not only calculation, but comparison, selection, arranging in sequence, sorting, recording and storing data, and making deductions from that data by logical rules. The data need not be in numerical form. It may be alphabetical or alphanumeric, as many of the specifications in an engineering stores system are. The necessary requirement is that the terms used in the data system are capable of definitions which can be related to the characteristics they measure or describe. Thus computers can be, and are, used for language translation, for abstracting of documents, for the compilation of contracts and for providing information services. The matching of needs expressed in terms which have previously been made known to the computer system is one of the elementary ways of using a computer which has sometimes found light-hearted expression in the work of a marriage bureau. The methods by which a computing system can be constructed to perform these operations need be of no concern to the manager. The fact that the methods exist is of concern.

When the word 'computer' is used, it is the giant computer of the cartoonists that is generally in mind. It is right that it should be so, for it is the giant that has the greatest potential ultimately for service to the manager. Such 'computers' are digital computing systems. There are, however, two types of computing systems—digital and analogue. Both are useful if used for the proper things and in the proper circumstances. What distinguishes them is the means by which the data for processing is represented in the system.

Analogue systems represent the data by a physical property. Thus, for instance, a thermometer represents the temperature of a body by the length of a column of mercury or other material and the changes in the quantity of heat by the contraction or expansion of the column. In another form, a thermometer linked to a control mechanism, as in a thermostat, becomes an analogue computing system capable of taking decisions and acting upon them. A slide rule is also an analogue computer, representing data by lengths on pieces of wood, in which calculations are performed by moving the pieces relatively to each other. Any physical property is available for use in analogue devices if means can be found for using it to represent data. Angles traced out by a pointer on a dial and electrical voltages are two further examples.

Analogue computers have the considerable advantage that they are fairly easy to design and can be constructed at relatively low

I*

cost. However, the accuracy that can be achieved is limited by the degree of accuracy with which the physical property can be measured. In equipment for general use this is not great, and it is often difficult to maintain the stability of the properties on which the analogue's working depends. Moreover, analogue computers are not very versatile.

Digital computing systems, by contrast, represent the data by discrete units and operate by counting the units. Every human being arrives in the world with a built-in digital computing system —his fingers and toes. From this he graduates to other digital devices—a frame of beads or a mechanical adding machine, for example. In these, the data is represented by the individual beads or the teeth on a set of cog-wheels. In each case the calculations are performed by manipulating the units and counting them in the various combinations that result. Digital computing systems have two main advantages over analogue systems. In the first place, they are much more versatile. The same general-purpose digital system can tackle a wide range of applications, whereas analogue systems are special purpose, constructed specifically for a particular application and not readily adaptable for others. Secondly, there is no theoretical limit to the degree of accuracy that can be achieved in a digital system by building into it more and more clocks of unit counting devices. The limit is set only by cost and the space available. On the other hand, there are disadvantages. Large digital systems have much more complicated designs and are more expensive than analogue. Moreover, although the output of the results of calculations can be in familiar form and easy to interpret, operating the systems requires a good deal of preliminary time and thought spent in preparing programmes for the machines to follow. The choice of analogue or digital must depend on the applications envisaged. Some new systems now being designed are hybrid, incorporating both analogue and digital elements.

Digital computing systems are of various types. A staff of human computers working with pencils and paper and using their brains and memories is a digital computing system. A single mechanical adding machine is a digital computer and a battery of them, along with their girl operators, is a digital computing system. Today, however, when a computer is discussed it is the electronic type that is generally meant. In this, the mode in which the data is represented is the electronic pulse.

It is from the use of electronics that the great speed associated with modern computers comes. This is the one aspect of computers with which everyone is familiar and certainly the achievements in this direction can hardly be exaggerated. The recurring failure to realize its full potential comes not from the inability of the computer manufacturer to harness the power of electronics but from the lack of understanding on the part of the user of the fact that the computer is part of a system, or from the designer's failure to take account of the problems of the interfaces.

The electronic digital computing system has two other important attributes. On the one hand, the power that provides its means of operation, the electrical current, is used also as the method of representing the data. This attribute has the same degree of importance in integrating the processing of data as the addition by James Watt of the principle of the governor to the harnessing of steam had in developing the factory system of the first industrial revolution. Electrical current is used as power in many adding machines, but leaving the measurement and calculation to use other forms of representation. The electro-mechanical equipment of earlier punched card data-processing systems went some distance towards combining motive power and measuring yardstick, but not all the way.

The second important additional attribute of the electronic digital computing system is the fact that, throughout the whole of such systems, moving parts are very few. The result is a very much higher degree of reliability than in mechanical or electro-mechanical systems. By this it is not meant to imply that things never go wrong with electronic systems. Far from it, but there is a very vital difference between the way things can go wrong in electronic systems and the way in which they can go wrong in mechanical systems. In the latter there may be faulty working and wrong results obtained, and it may not be at all apparent that this is so. A spindle wrongly aligned in an adding machine or a pin operating intermittently in a punched card tabulator can still give to the machine the appearance of performing satisfactorily, but the calculations will nevertheless go awry. With electronic equipment, by contrast, in the vast majority of cases when something goes wrong either the operation comes to a complete halt or the results that emerge are easily recognizable as wrong.

Faulty planning of a system will not prevent mistakes in an electronic system any more than in a mechanical system, but good systems planning will be more reliably supported by a wholly electronic system than by a wholly mechanical system. In all the large data processing systems in use, mechanical, electro-mechanical and electronic parts are to be found. Experience shows that the incidence of faults due to poor working of the equipment is always greatest with the mechanical parts and least with the electronic. Knowledge of this is of vital importance for the manager, both in the design of the system with which he chooses to operate and in his assessment of the reliability of the information which is provided to him by the system.

The last word of the title automatic electronic digital computing system to be considered is the word automatic. Most of the disappointment occasioned by the all-too-frequent cases of apparent poor performances of computing systems installed in recent years has been as a result of a failure to appreciate the significance of the word automatic in this context. Many of the data processing systems installed as 'computers' have not been automatic at all, or only partially so. Their performance has been perfectly satisfactory in terms of what they were really capable of achieving, but poor in terms of the expectations of those who were going to use them.

If, on setting out to work in the morning, one is currently walking from the house to the station and it is desired to speed up the process, there is nothing wrong with buying a bicycle. Anyone doing so will certainly succeed in shortening the journey time to the station, but he will not be so foolish as to imagine that he has acquired a motor car. He will fully expect to have to do some work in pedalling the bicycle and he will be well aware that there is a limit to the number of passengers that he can carry. The same is true of computing systems, of which there are many types. Large numbers of them fall short of being automatic systems but are none the worse for that. They are perfectly valid systems for the purposes for which they are designed. The trouble comes when it is supposed that they are automatic systems and attempts are made to use them as such. For non-automatic systems, the human beings in the system will be required to do much more work than for an automatic system. Equally, there are many things easily done in an automatic system which can be done only with very great difficulty or at a grossly uneconomic cost on a non-automatic system.

An automatic electronic digital computing system will include an automatic computer. Such a computer stores within itself the programme of instructions it has to follow. It is also provided with means whereby, on the recognition of defined symbols, it can move from one section of the programme to another, and with further means whereby it can itself alter its own instructions. An automatic electronic digital computing system possesses other automatic features.

Punched card mechanical systems are non-automatic systems. Even after the inclusion of many of the pieces of equipment to which the name computer is given, they still remain non-automatic. The transformation of the system to a 'computer' is achieved only by including in the system certain kinds of computer. A necessary, but by no means sufficient, condition for this to happen is that the punched card parts of the system must become unmistakably subsidiary to the computer. There can be no question of equality, far less superiority, between the punched card operations and the other operations if the system is to be genuinely automatic.

The difference between non-automatic and automatic operating can be seen by considering how certain parts of a payroll calculation are carried out, first on a punched card system with a non-automatic computer and then on a computer system. In the case of the former, the steps of the operation are as follows.

A pack of cards relating to one of the departments for which payrolls are to be prepared is fed into the computer. These cards have punched into them all the details appropriate to that department. The process of making the payroll calculations for that department is carried out in a manner that has been pre-determined, and is made known through the medium of other cards to the computer at the same time as the data is presented. The results for that department are printed out as appropriate. The setting up of the system, the presenting of the data and the instructions on how the operation is to be carried out by the computer will have required human hands to assist. The next department will now be handled in a similar way, with another pack of cards on which other different details will have been punched. If the process of calculating the payroll in this department is different from the first, then a separate set of instructions will be presented along with the data. Human assistance will again be necessary to restart the system. So it proceeds, department after department, with human intervention required to guide the transfer of operations from one set of calculations to the next. This intervention may consist merely of loading card feed hoppers with the packs of new cards and starting up the machines, but if the data arrives in random order it will also include the handling of a preliminary sorting operation before the main payroll calculations can start for each department. Alternatively, the data may be used for a number of different operations. The hours worked on different jobs, for instance, are available not only for the calculation of pay but also for the preparation of job-costing figures. In some applications the same data may be used for four or five operations. There will be different sets of instructions for each operation and, as each new operation is started, the appropriate set of instructions has to be fed into the machine and that data fed in anew. The tables show how these two types of activity proceed when non-automatic machines are being used.

Stage	By Departments Successively		By Processes Successively	
	Department	Process	Department	Process
1	1	1	1	1
2	2	1	1	2
3	3	1	1	3
4	1	2	2	1
5	2	2	2	2
⋮	⋮	⋮	⋮	⋮

In moving from one stage to the next in either form of the activity, human intervention is required and machine operations cannot proceed until this intervention is complete.

Where an automatic electronic digital computing system is in use, the activity is very different. As before, sets of instructions for all the processes to be followed have to be prepared in advance. This is where the similarity ends, for in this case the programmes of instructions are not fed in piecemeal. They are assembled together and fed in once and for all at the beginning of the operation. Moreover, the data can be accepted in random order. No preliminary sorting is necessary. The whole process is now carried on quite automatically with no further human intervention, even though the process may last many hours or even days. This is the general image of a 'computer' and, given that the computer is part of an automatic electronic digital computing system, it is a true image. Without the automatic feature it would not be so. Only if this is fully understood can disappointment for both owners and users of computers be avoided.

OPERATIONS PERFORMED

The astonishment and awe engendered by the quite genuinely astounding achievements of the systems described masks the fact that the operations performed are, in reality, basic and familiar. The name given to one of the earliest computers was Leo, standing for Lyons Electronic Office (see p. 38 above). This describes it exactly, whether the office be in the administrative block or in the factory or in the research laboratory. The conventional office provides clerical means of performing the functions, the other provides electronic means.

In both cases, the first decision must be to decide upon the languages in which business is to be conducted. In Paris this will be French, in Berlin it will be German, in London it will be English. The language chosen must satisfy three conditions. These are:

1 it must be a language in which it is possible to give clear expression to the ideas arising in the course of business;
2 it must be understandable by those using it;
3 it must be possible for results to be achieved by its use.

So long as the language in which business is conducted is the natural language of a sufficiently large number of those employed, then the three conditions can be fulfilled, since those who can speak it can express their ideas in it, understand the ideas of others expressed in it and think in it.

The language of the electronic office is the language of pulses. If the ordinary symbols of the alphabet and the numerals can be represented uniquely by patterns of pulses, then the first of the conditions is satisfied. That it is possible will be accepted if one recalls the use of the Morse Code. The familiar distress signal SOS in morse is $\cdots - - - \cdots$, dashes denoting a long buzz on a transmitter and dots denoting a short buzz.

This can be translated into pulse language by representing the dashes by the presence of a pulse during a period of time and the dots by the absence of a pulse. SOS in such a code then becomes 0 0 0 1 1 1 0 0 0, where the absence of a pulse is denoted by zeroes and the presence of a pulse by ones.

For ease in recognition, each group of three intervals when a pulse may be present or absent is separated from its neighbouring group, and the signal becomes 0 0 0   1 1 1   0 0 0.

The whole of a code can be built up from combinations of only two states—either a pulse being present or a pulse being absent. This 'twoness' defines the scale of the coding system as the binary scale, and it is the basis of most automatic electronic digital computing systems. If the number of time intervals in which a pulse may or may not be present is restricted to three, the number of unique combinations is limited, and modern systems make use of five, six, seven or eight 'pulse or no pulse' positions. It is not sufficient, however, to devise a theoretically suitable coding system if it can neither be understood nor used for any useful purpose. The building of equipment to harness the electronic pulses, and the design of circuitry to utilize them in order to make calculations and to apply the rules of logic, is the province of the electronic engineer. The human beings in the system, moreover, are unable to read patterns of pulses or to write them. They must be provided with more conventional forms for the information in the systems with which they are involved, and with means of translating pulse language into their own and vice versa. This is the field of the designer of peripheral equipment for computing systems. That all these designers and engineers have successfully performed their tasks is evidenced by the increasing number of computing systems operating with circuitry and equipment designed by them.

The peripheral equipment which translates information in common form into the language of pulses may consist of the following.

1 Equipment to punch holes into lengths of paper tape, causing suitable combinations of holes to be coded in when individual character keys on a key-board are punched. The holes permit light to pass through them and to fall upon a set of photo-electric cells. In this way a pattern of pulses is generated exactly conforming to the pattern of holes.

2 Equipment to punch holes into stacks of cards. The holes again operate photo-electrically or allow parts of a brush of wires to make contact with a cylinder behind the card and generate a pattern of pulses corresponding to the pattern of holes.

3 Scanning equipment to read characters or patterns printed on documents which generates patterns of pulses to represent the characters.

In one or other of these ways the information required is made available in the language which the electronic office system can use. In the clerical office system the equipment used for this is pencil, pen or typewriter, with the guiding influence provided by the human brain. In the corresponding equipment for the electronic system the human brain selects a key to be depressed for the punching operation, which then automatically punches the right pattern, or a human hand presents a document to the scanner which then generates the pattern.

The clerical office requires its in-trays on the desk. The characteristics of an in-tray are, or should be, that:

1 access to the information is immediate;

2 the information resides in it only temporarily;

3 it contains a relatively small amount of information.

The electronic office must be provided with its in-trays, and these are known as *immediate access stores*. They have exactly the same characteristics, with the added characteristics that after use, when the current has been switched off, the information in the immediate access store is lost, and also that the provision of such stores is expensive. These provide restraints, missing in the clerical office, which ensure that the immediate access stores are used efficiently.

Some information must be retained after use, and filing cabinets are provided for this purpose. Electronic filing cabinets are termed the *main store*. The information is magnetically stored and, in contrast to immediate access store, is not lost when the current is switched off. To balance this gain, however, there is an increase in the time taken to obtain information from the main store as compared with the immediate access store. Main stores in the electronic sense can be provided at much less expense than immediate access stores and, in most computing systems, are provided in much greater quantity as a result.

Filing cabinets in an office cannot be increased in number indefinitely. There comes a time when recourse has to be had to a central registry or archives, where information needed on much less frequent occasions can be stored. The counterpart in the electronic system is the *backing store*, which exists outside the central processing unit and may be packs of punched cards, sometimes reels of paper tape or more commonly reels of magnetic tape or disc packs. Being external to the central processing system, increasing the backing stores involves no increase in the size of the more costly central processor. On the other hand, access to information stored externally is not immediate. A messenger system requires to be organized to bring information from store to processor and return it to store after use. The equipment available to provide these channels of information ranges from single paper tape or card readers to small computers which carry out certain tasks on the information as slaves to the master system.

An office must be provided with an office manager to control operations. For the electronic office this is the control unit, which signals the routeing of the information in the system, its temporary or permanent resting places, and the times at which the various operations are to be performed upon it. In its most elementary state, the control unit allots jobs in strict rotation, completing the whole of one before starting another. Since no job ever requires all the elements of an office completely and simultaneously, the consequence is that for quite a substantial period of the time many of the parts of the system are not being used. The more efficient an office manager becomes, the more deft does he become in breaking the jobs down into their component parts and time-tabling the parts of the jobs in order to achieve greater machine utilization. The more sophisticated electronic office managers achieve the same thing by a process known as time-sharing, in which system many jobs can be done together on the computer during the same period of time.

The well run office has procedures to which it adheres and which have been prepared to cover all the work to be done. In the case of the electronic office, these procedures are the programmes of instructions which provide the routines for the control units to follow. Their importance is even greater for the electronic office than for its counterpart, since without them the computing system can achieve nothing, and, unless they are correct and comprehensive, results will be wrong.

Calculations are required in any modern office, clerical or electronic. In the clerical system these will be performed by the humans in the system, with or without aid. This must be paralleled in the electronic office, and is achieved by making an arithmetic unit as the centre of the processor. In the design of the circuitry to perform the calculations lies the skill of the designer. It is in the distinctive features of the arithmetic unit, along with the control unit, that the reputation of a computer lies.

The essentials of a clerical office can be listed as:

a language in which to conduct business;
means of providing information in correct form;
in-trays;
filing cabinets;
archives;
an office manager;
procedures;
means of doing calculations.

These elements, together with those persons involved in operating the system, are all that is necessary to achieve results. There is one proviso, however. The language in which the business is conducted must be the language of those involved in operating the system. Otherwise an interpreter must be provided.

Now, in the case of the electronic office, the language in which business is conducted is never the same as the language of the human beings operating the system. So whenever human beings are included in the system an interpreter must be provided. This interpreter is the output equipment which makes visible and comprehensible to the humans those results which are already available inside the system in the language of pulses. The equipment will normally be some form of printer operating by signals sent from the computer.

It must be remembered that the interpreter is a supernumerary, and only required when there are language problems. It must be remembered further that the only objective of all business activity is action based on decision. In the normal clerical office the language in which the decision-making process is carried out, the language of the human operators and the language of the action are all three the same. This is not so with the electronic office. The language of the action and the language of the humans is the same, but is different from the language of the decision-making process. This can be resolved, as has been said, by providing an interpreter in the form of printer output equipment, and this is what is normally done. There is, however, another method of resolving it, which is by removing the human beings from the system. It is not possible for the humans to learn the language of pulses, but it is possible to conduct the action in that language. This is the basis on which the introduction of control equipment and automation in industry in general proceeds. Such equipment functions on electronic signals which can be sent direct from the equipment which has analysed the data and made the deductions leading to the decisions which give rise to the actions.

For the manager who wishes to be numerate, an awareness of the characteristics of automatic electronic digital computing systems and the functions of the various elements which they comprise is very necessary. It will be apparent that *effective* use of the tools of numeracy on any significant scale is impossible without the use of computers, and the development of computers themselves is fostered by the desire to make use of sophisticated operational research techniques. The two have developed separately, are not linked, but nevertheless have a considerable interest in each other's progress.

The numerate manager must therefore concern himself with the implications of the advent of computers. That they are here to stay must be his first conclusion. The dangers today, however, arise not from reluctance to introduce computers but from an eagerness to ascribe to them powers which they do not possess. So much so that often anthropomorphism of the computer emerges. Election night in Britain brings phrases broadcast over radio and television such as: 'Let's see what the computer thinks now.', 'What has the computer got to say about the majority?' and many others. There are other similar occasions. 'Computer makes pay error' and 'Computer Channel swim succeeds' are only two of very many newspaper headlines of a similar nature which have appeared in the British press. Such comments are at best unthinking, and at worst dangerous. They are dangerous because they obscure the reality that cleverness in using computers is of human origin. The human being is not eliminated from an automatic system, but the timing of the part he plays is altered. He is needed at the commencement. He may well be eliminated from the later stages.

Failure to realize this, or a reluctance to accept it, often prevents the full potential of a computing system being deployed. This happens whenever existing systems are transferred to computer working without thought being taken as to possible changes in the system. This is not to say that there may not be some gain even in retaining existing systems for computer working. For example, in a typical departmental structure of operations, payroll calculations will be performed in one department, and extracts made from the payroll figures for the cost accounting department so that they can provide productivity and control statistics. Summaries of these in turn will be made available to planning and scheduling departments so that future programmes can be realistically prepared. It would certainly be perfectly possible to use a computer with advantage to do each of these tasks separately, providing the figures necessary for each of the three tasks as computer output from an earlier task. This would be to use the computer to perform the tasks in the same way as before. However, both the costing and planning requirements stem fundamentally from the payroll calculations, and to obtain the best use of a computer it would be preferable to provide them in parallel rather than in sequence.

There are other considerations for the manager to bear in mind.

1 Although a computer might be available, there are many jobs where it is much more economical to use more conventional equipment, assuming it is possible to have all the equipment one desires.

2 For many jobs it is more economical to use a large automatic electronic digital computing system than a small computer.

3 Responsibility for decision-making is not lost if responsibility for the processing of the data is handed over. The need to have access to the largest possible computing systems for economical working may require the data processing to be done at a computer service bureau rather than on one's own, probably smaller, system.

4 The types of systems that have been described are very inflexible systems. There can hardly be a single manager who has not been rescued from the consequences of his own instructions by his subordinates. No computing system will ever rescue a manager. His instructions will be carried out to the letter.

5 The task of the manager is to define meticulously what he wants done and the framework in which he wants it done, and to specify the limits and conditions he wishes to apply. The procedures and techniques required to *achieve* his objectives are matters for the experts.

6 Automatic electronic digital computing systems provide for the manager the opportunity to annihilate time, to annihilate distance and to annihilate error. The pictures of the moon's surface, obtained and made available on earth by such systems, must surely be convincing proof that this is so. The use made of the opportunity is the responsibility of the manager. His question need not now be 'Can it be done?' but 'How much is

it worth to me to have it done?' and 'How much will it cost to have it done?'

7 What the computer provides is speed. This in turn makes available

(a) time to do more of what one wants to do in a given time;

(b) the opportunity to use more accurate methods for certain operations which would have taken too long by other methods;

(c) the means of tackling problems impossible except by extremely sophisticated methods or without lengthy calculations.

Sometimes this speed is manifested through an ability to retain in the memory a vast quantity of data and to recall any of it in the minimum of time. At other times speed is provided through the ability to work through a complicated series of operations without losing track. Both objectives could be achieved by non-computer methods, but so slowly as to put the possibility of doing so right out of court.

The automatic electronic digital computing system is the equipment which makes possible the factory system of decision-making. It cannot be properly used until managers have an understanding of its nature and power. The numerate manager, more than any other, accepts this and takes steps to acquire the understanding.

PROGRAMMING THE COMPUTER

The availability of an electronic computer provides the opportunity, denied to earlier generations of decision-makers, of widening the scope and increasing the depth of the decision-making process. It provides for the human brain auxiliary thought-processing power, which will enable it to operate on much larger canvasses and to prepare much more complicated designs than the brain, unaided, could achieve. The use of an electronic computer, nevertheless, still requires the harnessing of human brain power to the tasks of making decisions. As in all forms of numerate decision-making, this comes at the earliest stage of the process, leaving the final stages to be performed by the use of automatic techniques.

When electronic computers are being used, there is an intermediate stage in which the design specifications prepared by the human brain are translated into forms suitable for feeding into the computer. Preparing the programmes of instructions (or *software* in the current jargon) which constitute these suitable forms is a matter for the specialists who will be assisting the decision-makers. Numerate managers can, however, acquire an understanding of the basic concepts of computer programming, and such an understanding will sharpen their appreciation of what is needed from them if the complete decision-making process is to be performed efficiently and, in particular, as economically as possible.

A stylized form of computer can be regarded as consisting of

1 a means of getting data and instructions into the computer;
2 an area where data and instructions are stored and where the results of instructions carried out on the data are also stored;
3 an area where the operations required by the instructions are carried out;
4 a means of getting the results out of the computer, either to perform required action directly or to be put into printed form for human interpretation.

The means of getting data and instructions into the computer will be some form of input device capable of reading paper-tape, punched cards, magnetic tape or documents. The storage area can be conceived of as consisting of a set of pigeon-holes in which characters, numerical or alphabetical, are located. As in storing verbal data on tapes used in tape-recorders, such characters reside in the locations in which they are placed until erased or replaced by other characters. Each storage location is identified by a unique address, and its size, which determines the amount of data it can hold, is something which the designer of the computer will have decided. Instructions are carried out in a unit capable of performing addition and subtraction and such other arithmetic and logical operations as the computer designer has decided are appropriate. Final results of operations are directed through an output unit to some chosen piece of auxiliary equipment, usually as yet a piece of printing equipment. A cypher has to be devised which can be interpreted by the computer so that data can be moved and operations performed as required. The interpretation is electronically carried out, the cyphered instructions, together with all relevant data, having first been put manually into suitable form.

One of the points of difference between one computer and another lies in the sophistication of the order codes to which they will respond. A primitive computer will incorporate circuitry to perform very few operations, and its order code will include very few instructions. The programmer must write the programme in terms of the instructions in the order code, and any operations required have to be described in terms of the operations which the computer can carry out. Thus, for instance, if the computer can perform the operation of multiplication the order code will contain an instruction of the form

multiply five by two

In this case the programmer need write one instruction only. If, on the other hand, the computer cannot perform the operation of multiplication, but can perform the operation of addition, multiplication is still possible. The programme of instructions will, however, be considerably longer. The steps now required will be of the following form:

> Set a signal at 'two'
> Set a counter to zero
> Add five to zero
> Note the result
> Add one to counter
> Check if counter is the same as signal
> If so, stop. If not, carry on.
> Add five to previous result
> Note new result
> Add one to counter
> Check if counter is the same as signal
> If so, stop. If not, carry on.

In this example, five was to be multiplied by two, and the counter would become the same as the signal after two sequences of instructions. With a larger multiplier very many more sequences of instructions would be required. It will be noticed that means must be available for recognizing the equality of two characters. In the case of numerals a zero answer to a subtraction sum provides such a means.

In writing a programme with such an order code, the programmer would soon observe that in the case of multiplication he was at liberty to use either number as the multiplier, and that his effort in writing instructions would be economized if he always used the smaller of the two as the multiplier. He would observe, too, that to write separate programmes every time he wanted to multiply, merely because the numbers involved were different, was a tedious business. He would come to the conclusion that the thought process which constitutes the framework of the programme was the same in every case, and that if he could replace the numbers in his programme by some universal description, such as the storage locations where they could be found, he need only write out one programme and utilize it every time he wished to do multiplication. All that would be necessary further would be to ensure that the right numbers for each application were in the specified storage locations when they were needed.

Other thoughts would enter his head, too. Noticing that all sequences of instructions were virtually the same, he might begin to wonder whether the designers of computers could not provide means by which computers could recognize this fact and save him the effort of transcribing the sequence more than once.

Finally, he would ask himself whether there might not somewhere be a computer using which he could condense the sequence of instructions into a single order. In the development of modern computers these desires have been met.

The order code provided is one of the factors influencing the choice of a computer and, while it is not necessary for the decision-maker using a computer to be familiar with it in detail, a knowledge of the types of instructions it contains will not be wasted.

There are certain basic instructions which would today be common ground to all order codes. They would be those concerned with getting data into the computer, placing specific pieces of information in specified locations in the memory store, performing simple arithmetic and transmitting information from specified locations to some form of printing device. More complicated operations, such as extracting square roots, might be included as single instructions, but the types of such operations included would vary from one computer to another, and would depend on the designer's view as to the needs of the users he was trying to satisfy. For the purposes of understanding the concepts of programming, the computer can be visualized as consisting of a set of pigeon-holes in which information is stored. As in operating a tape-recorder, the information placed in a pigeon-hole remains intact until either erased or over-written by other information. Once overwritten or erased, it is lost. It can be copied into another location and, again as in operating a tape-recorder, it remains intact in its original location. Each of the pigeon-holes is identified by an address, as shown.

0	1	2	3	4	5	6	7
8	9	10	11	12	13	14	15
16	17	18	19	20	21	22	23
24	25	26	27	28	29	30	31
32	33	34	35	36	37	38	39

The number of storage locations available and the amount of information that can be stored in each is important in considering the jobs to be put on the computer and the way they should be carried out. To this set of pigeon-holes is attached an input channel, an arithmetic unit and a printing device. The actual symbols used for coding the instructions is a matter of choice. The way in which a programme can be built up is best seen by following an example in which the order code being used contains these instructions:

Instruction	Interpretation
$s_n = \text{Tape } p$	Read p numbers from paper-tape into store starting at storage location n
$s_n = XYZ$	Store number XYZ in storage location n
$s_n = s_a + s_b$	Add number in storage location a to number in storage location b and copy the answer into storage location n
$s_n = s_a - s_b$	Subtract number in storage location b from number in storage location a and copy the answer in storage location n
$s_n = s_a \times s_b$	Multiply number in storage location a by number in storage location b and copy the answer in storage location n
$s_n = s_a \div s_b$	Divide number in storage location a by number in storage location b and copy the answer in storage location n
$s_n = s_a$	Copy the number in storage location a into storage location n
Print s_n	Print out the contents of storage location n
$\rightarrow X)$	Jump unconditionally to the section of the programme starting with the instruction labelled X)
$\rightarrow X), s_n = y$	Jump to the section of the programme starting with the instruction labelled X) if the contents of storage location n are equal to y
STOP	Stop operations

Suppose the calculation of a standard cost is to be programmed for a computer to which the order code applies. The process of calculating the standard cost is specified as follows.

For each of the many processes that occur a labour cost is

calculated, by multiplying the hours worked on the process by the hourly rate applicable to that operation. A material cost is obtained by applying a wastage factor to the recipe quantity of the material, and the corrected quantity multiplied by the unit cost of that raw material. The labour cost and the material cost are added together to give the total cost for that process. This calculation is repeated for each process, and the results of the calculations added together. This total is divided by the total of the recipe quantities of the materials used. The operation is denoted symbolically as follows:

Let $q_1, q_2, q_3, \ldots$ be the recipe quantities of the ingredients in processes 1, 2, 3, $\ldots$

$w_1, w_2, w_3, \ldots$ be the wastage factors respectively

$c_1, c_2, c_3, \ldots$ be the material unit cost respectively

$h_1, h_2, h_3, \ldots$ be the hours worked on each process respectively

r_1, r_2, r_3 be the hourly labour rates paid for each process respectively

Then if c be the required standard cost

$$c = \frac{[h_1 r_1 + q_1(1 + w_1)c_1] + [h_2 r_2 + q_2(1 + w_2)c_2] + \ldots}{q_1 + q_2 + \ldots}$$

or

$$c = \frac{\sum\limits_{n=1}^{p} [h_n r_n + q_n(1 + w_n)c_n]}{\sum\limits_{n=1}^{p} q_n}$$

where p is the number of processes in the operation.

The significance of the instructions will emerge more clearly as the programme is developed. Initially the data has to be put in position for the calculation to proceed, and the first instruction required, therefore, is a READ instruction. The calculation of the cost of each process involves five pieces of data, h, r, q, w and c. The five pieces of data relating to the first process will be at the commencement of the data tape. For a reason which will emerge later, each group of five pieces of data is accompanied by a sixth character, which will be one particular character if there is a further set of data to follow on the data tape, and a different character if there is no more data to follow. Suppose an asterisk is used as the character to indicate that there is more data to follow on the data tape, and the absence of an asterisk as the sixth of each group of six characters indicates that there is no further data to follow.

The first six pieces of data, then, are h, r, q, w, c, *. These must be stored in the computer memory, and it is for the programmer to specify which locations he wishes to use and, no doubt, he will start by using the first locations to hand. The first instruction, therefore, is

$$s_0 = \text{Tape 6}$$

When this instruction has been obeyed, the state of the memory is as shown.

0	1	2	3	4	5	6	7
h_1	r_1	q_1	w_1	c_1	*		

All the data for the calculation of the cost of the first process is now stored in the computer memory, except that a factor $1+w_1$ is needed rather than w_1. This the programmer can achieve with two consecutive instructions.

$$s_6 = 1$$

will place the number 1 in storage location 6, and

$$s_7 = s_6 + s_3$$

will add together the contents of storage locations 6 and 3 and place the result $(1+w_1)$ in storage location 7.

The programme now reads

$$s_0 = \text{Tape 6}$$
$$s_6 = 1$$
$$s_7 = s_6 + s_3$$

and the state of the memory is as shown.

0	1	2	3	4	5	6	7
h_1	r_1	q_1	w_1	c_1	*	1	$1+w_1$

The first calculation required is the labour cost, obtained by multiplying h_1 by r_1. h_1 is in s_0 and r_1 is in s_1. The instruction

$$s_8 = s_0 \times s_1$$

will achieve this and put the result in s_8.

The state of the programme and memory are now as shown.

$$s_0 = \text{Tape } 6$$
$$s_6 = 1$$
$$s_7 = s_6 + s_3$$
$$s_8 = s_0 \times s_1$$

0 h_1	1 r_1	2 q_1	3 w_1	4 c_1	5 *	6 1	7 $1+w_1$
8 $h_1 r_1$	9	10	11	12	13	14	15

Also needed is the material cost $q_1(1+w_1)c_1$. The order code does not permit three numbers to be multiplied together in one instruction. This has to be achieved in two steps.

$$s_9 = s_2 \times s_7$$

will put $q_1(1+w_1)$ into s_9

0 h_1	1 r_1	2 q_1	3 w_1	4 c_1	5 *	6 1	7 $1+w_1$
8 $h_1 r_1$	9 $q_1(1+w_1)$	10	11	12	13	14	15

while the next instruction

$$s_{10} = s_9 \times s_4$$

will put $q_1(1+w_1)c_1$ into s_{10}

0 h_1	1 r_1	2 q_1	3 w_1	4 c_1	5 *	6 1	7 $1+w_1$
8 $h_1 r_1$	9 $q_1(1+w_1)$	10 $q_1(1+w_1)c_1$	11	12	13	14	15

What is required now is to add together the labour cost $h_1 r_1$ and the material cost $q_1(1+w_1)c_1$ to give the total cost for the first process.

$$s_{11} = s_8 + s_{10}$$

will achieve this and store the result in s_{11}.

0 h_1	1 r_1	2 q_1	3 w_1	4 c_1	5 *	6 1	7 $1+w_1$
8 h_1r_1	9 $q_1(1+w_1)$	10 $q_1(1+w_1)c_1$	11 h_1r_1+ $q_1(1+w_1)c_1$	12	13	14	15

This is the calculation for the first process completed. The programme now reads

$$s_0 = \text{Tape 6}$$
$$s_6 = 1$$
$$s_7 = s_6+s_3$$
$$s_8 = s_0 \times s_1$$
$$s_9 = s_2 \times s_7$$
$$s_{10} = s_9 \times s_4$$
$$s_{11} = s_8+s_{10}$$

To carry out the calculation for the second process, the next 6 pieces of data on the data tape need to be read into the store. The instruction

$$s_{12} = \text{Tape 6}$$

would achieve this, and the data would be stored as follows

$$h_2 \text{ in } s_{12}$$
$$r_2 \text{ in } s_{13}$$
$$q_2 \text{ in } s_{14}$$
$$w_2 \text{ in } s_{15}$$
$$c_2 \text{ in } s_{16}$$
$$* \text{ in } s_{17}$$

The programme could proceed with the same sequence of instructions repeated as before. Now, however, each address of the storage locations is 12 greater than in the first sequence. The state of the memory after this second sequence had been repeated would be as shown.

0 h_1	1 r_1	2 q_1	3 w_1	4 c_1	5 *	6 1	7 $1+w_1$
8 h_1r_1	9 $q_1(1+w_1)$	10 $q_1(1+w_1)c_1$	11 h_1r_1+ $q_1(1+w_1)c_1$	12 h_2	13 r_2	14 q_2	15 w_2
16 c_2	17 *	18 1	19 $1+w_2$	20 h_2r_2	21 $q_2(1+w_2)$	22 $q_2(1+w_2)c_2$	23 h_2r_2+ $q_2(1+w_2)c_2$

The programmer would have to take careful note that $q_1, q_2, q_3, \ldots$ of which he requires the sum for the denominator are stored in $s_2, s_{14}, s_{26} \ldots$ Similarly the total costs of each process, the sum of which is required for the numerator are stored in $s_{11}, s_{23}, s_{35}, \ldots$. The programmer would be compelled to restrict the number of processes to be calculated by the programme to keep the number of locations required within the number provided in the computer memory. The number of instructions necessary for a programme to be used in a manufacturing operation with numerous processes would be somewhat tedious to prepare.

Fortunately, in the order code being used there is a means of overcoming these nuisances. The key lies in the use of a jump instruction.

If the first instruction of the sequence is given a label 1), and an additional instruction

$$\rightarrow 1)$$

is added at the end of the sequence, the programme now has the appearance

$$
\begin{aligned}
1) \quad s_0 &= \text{Tape 6} \\
s_6 &= 1 \\
s_7 &= s_6 + s_3 \\
s_8 &= s_0 \times s_1 \\
s_9 &= s_2 \times s_7 \\
s_{10} &= s_9 \times s_4 \\
s_{11} &= s_8 + s_{10} \\
&\rightarrow 1)
\end{aligned}
$$

This has the effect of causing the computer to return to the beginning of the sequence and to obey once again the set of instructions in the same order as before. When the final instruction has once more been obeyed, the state of the memory is now as shown.

0	1	2	3	4	5	6	7
h_2	r_2	q_2	w_2	c_2	*	1	$1+w_2$

8	9	10	11	12	13	14	15
$h_2 r_2$	$q_2(1+w_2)$	$q_2(1+w_2)c_2$	$h_2 r_2 + q_2(1+w_2)c_2$				

The new data overwrites the old data, and each step in the calculation replaces the old intermediate results with the new. The final step in the calculation stores in s_{11} the total cost for the second process. This is what is required, but it will be apparent immediately that, in obtaining it, the cost for the first process has been lost, along with all the first process data. Now, although the data is no longer needed, the total cost must not be lost, and the programmer is faced with the problem of ensuring that it is not lost. This consideration applies with equal force to q_1 which is needed in the denominator.

A first thought might be that the result can be saved by copying the contents of s_{11} and s_2 into, say, s_{12} and s_{13} before obeying the Jump Instruction. A moment's reflection, however, will show that exactly the same thing will happen in s_{12} and s_{13} as in s_{11} and s_2. The copying instructions

$$s_{12} = s_{11}$$

and $$s_{13} = s_2$$

will therefore not bring success.

Further thought will remind the programmer that he does not, in fact, require the individual costs of each process and the quantity of each material used, but the summation of these figures to give the numerator and the denominator respectively. If, therefore, instead of merely copying each successive content of s_{11} and s_2 into s_{12} and s_{13} respectively, it is added to what is already there, then these summations will be accumulated each time the computer goes round the loop of instructions.

Thus, the instructions needed are

$$s_{12} = s_{12} + s_{11}$$
$$s_{13} = s_{13} + s_2$$

The programme is now

$$
\begin{aligned}
1)\quad s_0 &= \text{Tape 6} \\
s_6 &= 1 \\
s_7 &= s_6 + s_3 \\
s_8 &= s_0 \times s_1 \\
s_9 &= s_2 \times s_7 \\
s_{10} &= s_9 \times s_4 \\
s_{11} &= s_8 + s_{10} \\
s_{12} &= s_{12} + s_{11} \\
s_{13} &= s_{13} + s_2 \\
&\rightarrow 1)
\end{aligned}
$$

and the state of the memory is now as shown after going round the loop the first time

0 h_1	1 r_1	2 q_1	3 w_1	4 c_1	5 *	6 1	7 $1+w_1$
8 h_1r_1	9 $q_1(1+w_1)$	10 $q_1(1+w_1)c_1$	11 h_1r_1+ $q_1(1+w_1)c_1$	12 Numerator	13 Denomi- nator	14	15

What the programmer has now provided is a set of instructions which will cause the computer to read in the set of data relevant to a particular process, do the cost calculations and accumulate the results. This it will do for each process in succession, automatically jumping at the right time to the instruction which will cause it to read in the next set of data. What the programmer has not yet provided is a means by which the computer will stop going round the loop of instructions.

To achieve this the unconditional jump instruction which has so far been included in the programme is replaced by a conditional jump instruction. It is in this context that the sixth character in each section of data has significance. It will be remembered that this sixth character was always to be * if there was more data to follow. The conditional jump instruction that is needed, therefore, is

$$\rightarrow 1), s_5 = *$$

The programme now becomes

$$1) \quad s_0 = \text{Tape 6}$$
$$s_6 = 1$$
$$s_7 = s_1 + s_3$$
$$s_8 = s_0 \times s_1$$
$$s_9 = s_2 \times s_7$$
$$s_{10} = s_9 \times s_4$$
$$s_{11} = s_8 + s_{10}$$
$$s_{12} = s_{12} + s_{11}$$
$$s_{13} = s_{13} + s_2$$
$$\rightarrow 1), s_5 = *$$

The programme will now ensure that the loop of instructions is not obeyed when there is no more data to come. The calculation now needed is to divide the numerator by the denominator, which provides the standard cost per unit as the final result. The result must then be printed out and two further instructions achieve this

$$s_{14} = s_{12} \div s_{13}$$
$$\text{PRINT } s_{14}$$

Lastly a positive instruction to the computer to stop operations should be included.

The programme finally becomes

$$
\begin{aligned}
1) \quad s_0 &= \text{Tape } 6 \\
s_6 &= 1 \\
s_7 &= s_6 + s_3 \\
s_8 &= s_0 \times s_1 \\
s_9 &= s_2 \times s_7 \\
s_{10} &= s_9 \times s_4 \\
s_{11} &= s_8 + s_{10} \\
s_{12} &= s_{12} + s_{11} \\
s_{13} &= s_{13} + s_2 \\
\rightarrow 1), \; s_5 &= * \\
s_{14} &= s_{12} \div s_{13} \\
&\text{PRINT } s_{14} \\
&\text{STOP}
\end{aligned}
$$

The programmer would not, of course, leave it there. There are many ways in which he would improve it so that its running time would be shortened. One obvious step he could take would be to take the instruction $s_6 = 1$ out of the loop, since when it has been obeyed once it has served its purpose for all the processes in the costing operation. In improving the programme, no new concepts would be included, and it is with the concepts only that the manager need be concerned.

What is important is the realization that a change to a computer system is not merely a case of installing a piece of equipment. It involves a rethinking of aims and methods of operation and, for greater success, an understanding of what is included in the very necessary preparation for any computer operation.

CHAPTER V

SOME CHARACTERISTICS OF INFORMATION

An understanding of the equipment is a necessary condition for efficient handling of information. It is not, however, sufficient. Two further areas of understanding have to be covered. These are:

1 an understanding of the characteristics of data and information;
2 an understanding of the characteristics of reasoning.

Data can be defined as things given. Things given need not necessarily inform. Much of the vast mass of data does not inform. One reason for this is its vastness, since data includes everything recorded or discovered. Even with computers, this is unmanageable and means have to be found of choosing a relatively small number of representatives for the data. These must be such as will effectively offer the same characteristics as the data itself.

CHOICE OF REPRESENTATIVE

The best known representative where the data is numerical is the average or mean. It has the merit of being easy to calculate and for this reason is widely used. If the use made of it is for further calculations this is perfectly valid. Thus, for instance, the average salary paid can quite correctly be used as a multiplier for the number of people on the payroll in order to provide a salary budget for the whole organization. It can only be used, however, where numerical values can be applied to the objects being considered and where these have some meaning for the type of calculation to be done.

Suppose that there are in a certain department in a factory three machines, whose hourly rates of output are 200, 1000 and 1100 parts respectively. Staff is available to work only one machine in the week ahead. The arithmetic average output per machine is 800 parts per hour, and this is shown in returns as the average performance for the department. Although it would be correct to use 800

as a basis for calculating the additional total output of the department if, say, six hours overtime were worked on all machines, it
would be wrong to use that figure for a decision concerning, say,
supplies needed to meet the production needs of the single machine
operating during the following week.

In calculating a plain arithmetic average, extreme values which
are well out of line with all the rest count for just as much as any
other. The result is that the arithmetic average gives a distorted
representation of the bulk of the values. This consequence can be
ameliorated by assigning degrees of importance or weight to the
values, each of the values then being multiplied by its weight before
adding it in to the total. The result is a weighted average which, if
the weights are well chosen, will reduce the distortion caused by
extreme values. If there is a truly objective method of choosing the
values for the weighting factors, then a weighted average is a good
representative for decision-making purposes. However, such methods
are not easy to find.

For decision-making, though not for use in calculations, two
better representatives than either the arithmetic average or an
uncertainly weighted average are often the median and the mode.
Of the two, the median can be more easily obtained.

Suppose a manufacturer of collars for men decides to standardize
his production on one collar size. Which one shall it be? To help
him in his decision-making, he obtains information from the market
that in every hundred people the number who buy collars of various
sizes is given in the following table:

Collar Size	Number of People
12	3
12½	4
13	6
13½	6
14	8
14½	11
15	16
15½	17
16	15
16½	8
17	6

To obtain the median, the measurements are arranged in some
convenient sequence. In this case the most convenient sequence is
ascending order of collar size, as has been done in the table. If all

the observations are arranged in such a sequence, it will be noticed that there are 38 observations of collar size less than size 15, and 46 observations of collar size greater than 15. The median, as its name implies, is the middle observation. If there is an odd number of observations, the middle observation is uniquely defined; if there is an even number of observations, then two middle observations are available for choice. The value is then taken to be the average of the values of these two middle observations.

In this case, the middle observations are the 50th and 51st, and the value of each is size 15. The median is therefore size 15.

If the manufacturer accepted the median as the best representative, he would standardize his production on size 15 collars. It will be noticed that in this example the median and the arithmetic average of the collar sizes are the same. But the median takes less time to find.

Consider, on the other hand, market information as given in this table. In this case nobody buys sizes 15 and $15\frac{1}{2}$, perhaps because fashion has decreed that youths of the age group which would normally wear those sizes should wear cravats instead of collars.

Collar Size	Number of People
13	6
$13\frac{1}{2}$	6
14	8
$14\frac{1}{2}$	11
16	15
$16\frac{1}{2}$	8
17	6

In this case the median is $14\frac{1}{2}$, while the arithmetic average is 15 to the nearest half size. It should be noticed that in both these examples the median represents a measurement which has actually been observed, while the arithmetic average in the second example does not. Thus a decision based on the median will exactly suit some people, while a decision to standardize on size 15 in the second example will exactly suit nobody.

A study of the information in the first table will reveal that even more people would have been exactly suited if the decision had been taken to standardize on size $15\frac{1}{2}$ instead of size 15. By taking into account the number of occurrences of each measurement, it can be determined which of the measurements occurs most frequently. This is the mode or most fashionable measurement.

Decisions based on the mode will give exact satisfaction in at least as many, and usually more, cases than decisions based on any other representative of a set of data.

MEASURE OF RELIABILITY

The best representative having been chosen, it is necessary to know how reliable it is as a basis for decision-making. The method of measuring reliability introduces the statistical concept of deviation. The deviation of any measurement is simply the difference between the numerical value of that measurement and the numerical value of whatever representative is being used. In taking these differences the sign is ignored, since plus deviations and minus deviations are of equal interest and importance. From these deviations a measure of reliability can be formed, by taking their average. This is known as the mean deviation. More commonly, however, the deviations are first squared and the average taken of the squares. The square root of this average provides a measure of reliability which is known as the root-mean-square deviation. When the deviations are measured from the arithmetic average of the observations, the root-mean-square deviation is given the special name of standard deviation, and is denoted by the Greek letter σ. If x is the observation and m the mean of all the observations, the standard deviation can be calculated from the formula

$$\sigma = \sqrt{\frac{\sum(x-m)^2}{n}}$$

Since it can be shown that a relationship exists between the root-mean-square deviation, when deviations are calculated from representatives other than the mean, and the standard deviation, the latter is always used in normal practice.

The results of following this process are shown in this example, each measurement being counted as often as the number of times it was found.

Putting the values $n = 100$ and $\sum(x-m)^2 = 646/4$ into the formula

$$\sigma = \sqrt{\frac{\sum(x-m)^2}{n}}$$

gives a value for the standard deviation of 1·3.

Representative—15(mean)

(1) Measurement	(2) No.	(3) Deviation	(4) (Deviation)^2	(2) × (4)
12	3	3	36/4	108/4
12½	4	2½	25/4	100/4
13	6	2	16/4	96/4
13½	6	1½	9/4	54/4
14	8	1	4/4	32/4
14½	11	½	1/4	11/4
15	16	nil	nil	—
15½	17	½	1/4	17/4
16	15	1	4/4	60/4
16½	8	1½	9/4	72/4
17	6	2	16/4	96/4

$$\Sigma(x-m)^2 = 646/4$$

Standard deviation (or root-mean-square deviation) is important for a number of reasons.

First, it provides a measure of comparison of the reliability of representatives of different sets of data.

Secondly, for certain patterns of observations it provides a means of estimating how great a tolerance has to be applied to the representative in taking decisions. In practice, decisions are not taken to act in a precise value, but rather over a range of values. It becomes important to know how wide the range should be in order that any given proportion of the target population should be encompassed. If the pattern of observations is such that it is reasonably symmetrical about its average, and if the maximum number of occurrences of values is concentrated round a single value, then a good rough-and-ready rule to follow states that two thirds of the distribution will lie less than one standard deviation away from the representative. In the example above, for instance, the mean was 15 and the standard deviation 1·3. To encompass two thirds of the purchasers of collars would require a decision to manufacture collars of sizes 14, 14½, 15, 15½ and 16. If the numbers are extracted from the table, it will be found that this, in fact, is 67 per cent. The tolerances needed for other proportions of the target can now be worked out. It can be shown, for instance, that less than 1 per cent of the distribution will lie more than three standard deviations away from the mean.

Thirdly, where decisions are based not on all observations, but on a sample of them, as is usually the case in business decision-making, it becomes important to know also the degree of error inherent in the sample. The concept of standard deviation is used to arrive at a margin of error which should be assigned to a particular estimate. Market research may show, for example, that potential purchasers of one's product number 6,000,000, and from the standard deviation of the sampling distribution it may be calculated that the margin of error is $2\frac{1}{2}$ per cent. In practice, therefore, in formulating decisions there is no reason to take any number between 5,850,000 and 6,150,000 as being sounder than any other. The calculation of tolerances and standard errors is a matter for the statistician, but a knowledge of their existence, and an appreciation of the concept of standard deviation on which they are based, will enable the numerate manager to ask the right questions of his statistical experts.

PROBABILITY

There is always a factor of uncertainty in the handling of data relating to business decisions. That chance has a hand in affairs sometimes leads to the view that statistical manipulation and the use of mathematical techniques of interpretation is a pointless exercise. This should not be the view of the numerate manager, who certainly accepts that all data is subject to chance influences but who, in addition, attempts to measure the effect of those influences.

In assessing data, four distinct influences must be considered. These are:

1 local fluctuations;
2 trends;
3 chance;
4 causative factors.

Local fluctuations consist typically of seasonal effects on the data as, for instance, summer peaks in the sale of ice cream or winter peaks in the sale of tinned soups. Others may be due in the long term to fluctuations in demand caused by changes in the level of employment, for instance, or by variations in the balance of payments. Statistical account can be taken of such fluctuations. Smoothing techniques will remove from the data their effects.

Also affecting the data will be a number of economic trends whose existence is known and whose influence can be calculated. By a number of statistical devices these too can be removed, leaving the data now free of the variations due to local fluctuations and long-term trends.

What the manager wishes to know is whether the variations which are now left in the data are due to some specific cause or causes whose nature he should try to discover. Before he draws any conclusions, however, he needs to know whether the variations are such as could occur by pure chance alone. Some knowledge of how chance factors operate is therefore desirable.

The purest chance situation that exists is the tossing of a coin, possessing two sides that are different in design—a heads and a tails. It would be generally accepted that in each tossing of such a coin the chances of the coin coming down heads would be the same as the chances of it coming down tails. Some recent investigations have shown that in clinical conditions where the force and direction of tossing can be repeated exactly time after time, minute differences in the amount of metal left after the designs have been etched may provide a bias in favour of one side or another. In normal circumstances clinical conditions cannot be reproduced, and such a fine distinction can be ignored. In probability theory, absolute certainty is 1. Therefore the probability of getting a head in a single toss is $\frac{1}{2}$, and the probability of getting a tail in a single toss is $\frac{1}{2}$.

Another way of expressing the situation is to say that in a large number of tossings 50 per cent of them will come down heads and 50 per cent of them will come down tails. This latter method of expressing it is normally the more useful for understanding the working of chance in business problems.

This result would be arrived at intuitively in the case of a single trial with a single coin. Suppose, instead, four coins were tossed

	1st coin	2nd coin	3rd coin	4th coin
4 heads—1 way	H	H	H	H
3 heads—4 ways	H	H	H	T
	H	H	T	H
	H	T	H	H
	T	H	H	H
2 heads—6 ways	H	H	T	T
	H	T	H	T
	T	H	H	T
	H	T	T	H
	T	T	H	H
	T	H	T	H
1 head—4 ways	H	T	T	T
	T	H	T	T
	T	T	H	T
	T	T	T	H
0 heads—1 way	T	T	T	T

simultaneously. What would be the chances of getting four heads, three heads, two heads, one head and no head respectively? The probabilities can be found by listing all the ways in which the coins can fall. This is as shown on the previous page.

There are sixteen possible ways in which the coins can fall. In only one of these ways is a four-head result obtained. So the probability of obtaining four heads in a throw of four coins is 1/16. Similarly for the other patterns the probabilities are:

3 heads	4/16
2 heads	6/16
1 head	4/16
0 heads	1/16

Alternatively the result can be described by saying that in 16,000 operations one could expect

1,000 to be 4 heads
4,000 to be 3 heads
6,000 to be 2 heads
4,000 to be 1 head
1,000 to be 0 heads

It will be noticed that the result is symmetrical, and a little thought will show that this must be so. The argument could have been developed by using the word 'tail' wherever 'head' was used previously and 'head' wherever 'tail' was used. The only way in which the two arguments can be consistent is if the probabilities conform to a statistical pattern.

By similar arguments one can develop that for three tossings the probabilities are in the ratio 1   3   3   1

for five tossings   1   5   10   10   5   1
for six tossings   1   6   15   20   15   6   1.

It can be shown that in mathematical terms the ratios of the probabilities of the various combinations that can occur in n tossings are given by the coefficients in the binomial expansion of $(a+b)^n$. This expansion is

$$a^n + na^{n-1}b + \frac{n(n-1)}{2 \cdot 1}a^{n-2}b^2 + \frac{n(n-1)(n-2)}{3 \cdot 2 \cdot 1}a^{n-3}b^3 + \ldots$$

$$\ldots + \frac{n(n-1)(n-2) \ldots 2}{(n-1)(n-2) \ldots 2 \cdot 1}ab^{n-1} + \frac{n(n-1)(n-2) \ldots 2 \cdot 1}{n(n-1)(n-2) \ldots 2 \cdot 1}b^n$$

These coefficients form the pattern

$$1, n, \frac{n(n-1)}{2.1}, \frac{n(n-1)(n-2)}{3.2.1}, \ldots \frac{n(n-1)\ldots 2}{(n-1)(n-2)\ldots 2.1}, \frac{n(n-1)\ldots 2.1}{n(n-1)\ldots 2.1}$$

n takes a value given by the number of tossings.

Thus for one tossing the pattern becomes   1   1
      for two tossings the pattern becomes   1   2   1
      for three tossings the pattern becomes   1   3   3   1
      for four tossings the pattern becomes   1   4   6   4   1
      and so on as before.

To obtain the probabilities, each of these figures is divided by the total in its pattern. The denominator for one tossing is 2, giving probabilities of a head as $\frac{1}{2}$, and not-a-head as $\frac{1}{2}$, as before.

      For two tossings the denominator is   4
      For three tossings the denominator is   8
      For four tossings the denominator is   16

It will be noticed that the denominator is the total number of ways in which the coins can fall.

These results could be shown graphically. When there are only a few occurrences or possibilities the results would be presented as a bar chart or histogram. With a larger number of occurrences the outline would take on more and more the appearance of a continuous curve and would be bell-shaped.

This is the normal pattern for all curves of such chance occurrences. Hence it is known as the normal curve of distribution. The occurrences in real life will not be the tossings of coins, but they may be any event which either happens or does not happen. The events may relate to the purchase of various quantities of some particular product, for instance, or to the purchase or non-purchase of an article at various prices. They may also relate to the values obtained as a result of measuring some dimension in a fabricated product or to faults occurring in a component. If the events are under the influence of chance alone and each occasion is truly independent of every other occasion, then in each of the situations mentioned above, and in many others, the normal curve of distribution applies and can throw light on the way in which chance factors operate.

L

The importance of the normal curve lies in the fact that it can be expressed as a mathematical equation. This equation is of the form

$$y = \frac{1}{\sigma 2\pi} e^{-x^2/2\sigma^2}$$

e being the exponential, and from this the number of occurrences, y, of any event, x, can be calculated. The σ in the equation is the familiar standard deviation. Thus, for instance, as was stated earlier, it can be shown that a range of values extending from a lower limit of σ below the mean (which in the case of the normal curve is the same as the mode and the median) to an upper limit of σ above the mean will include roughly two thirds of all the occurrences. If the range is extended to 3σ above and below the mean, it will include all but a negligible number. More importantly, the calculation can be done in reverse to give an indication of how far a range of values has to be taken on either side of the mean for any given percentage of the observations under consideration to be included. The importance of this for the decision-maker, faced with a situation in which he has to allow for chance, is that he will not be working entirely in the dark. The most familiar practical application of this theory occurs in the setting of limits of tolerances in manufacturing operations and to decide upon the right size of samples to choose for inspection.

Not every pattern of chance approximates to a normal curve. One which does is the distribution of errors, and it is for this reason that the theory can be used in quality control work. The starting point for the mathematical development of the normal curve was that the probability of an event occurring is the same as the probability of the event not occurring. This is so, of course, in the tossing of a coin. Under certain conditions the normal curve would obtain if these probabilities were not equal. It does not apply where one of the probabilities is very small. In this case, however, another expression, first published by Poisson in 1837, has been found to apply. Poisson's distribution is of the form

$$e^{-m}(1 + m + \frac{m}{1 \cdot 2} + \frac{m^2}{1 \cdot 2} + \frac{m^3}{1 \cdot 2 \cdot 3 \cdot} + \text{etc.})$$

In this formula the e is a mathematical constant like the better known π. It was the base on which Napier developed the first logarithms. Like π its value cannot be completely determined, but for practical purposes it can be calculated to whatever number of decimal places are considered necessary. To four decimal places, its value is 2·7183.

In using the formula, m represents the average number of occurrences of the event in which interest is taken.

$e^{-m} \times 1$ then represents the probability of 0 events

$e^{-m} \times m$ then represents the probability of 1 event

$e^{-m} \times \dfrac{m^2}{1 \cdot 2}$ then represents the probability of 2 events

$e^{-m} \times \dfrac{m^3}{1 \cdot 2 \cdot 3}$ then represents the probability of 3 events

and so on.

Again, the value of such an expression lies in the fact that various deductions as to the consequences can be calculated mathematically. In theory it would be possible to fit mathematical equations to various patterns of chance, but these remain of academic interest only, unless the equations can be put in a form leading to answers to practical questions. In practice, normal and Poisson distributions are the types of most practical value.

With an understanding of the workings of chance and the use of a number of statistical techniques the influences of local fluctuations, trend and chance on a set of data can be measured and removed. For the remaining fluctuations other explanations must be sought from hitherto unknown causes. For the decision-maker it is important that he should be able to identify the nature of these causes as exactly as he can. The likelihood of his doing so is increased if the data, which is his evidence of their existence, is as realistic as possible. To make it so is the purpose of identifying and eliminating the other influences. Numeracy involves an awareness of the need to do so and of the possibility of doing it.

Normally the decision-maker will be faced with very many sets of data. Each of these he may consider independently and base his decisions on conclusions drawn from each. With some sets, however, he will be concerned to discover whether any relationship exists between them and whether there is an association between movements in one set and movements in another.

Measures of the strength of any relationships that exist can be derived by purely analytical means. If the means of the two sets of variables are found, then for each pair of variables the product of the deviations from their respective means can be found. If these are summed and their arithmetic average calculated, the result is a measure, r, known as the coefficient of correlation between the variables.

$$r = \frac{1}{N} \sum \frac{x - \bar{x}}{\sigma_x} \times \frac{y - \bar{y}}{\sigma_y}$$

Where N is the number of pairs of observations, $\bar{x}$ and $\bar{y}$ are the respective means, σ_x and σ_y are the standard deviations, $x - \bar{x}$ and $y - \bar{y}$ are the deviations of each value of x and y respectively. The correlation coefficient r must vary between -1 and $+1$. If r has either of these two values, the variables are perfectly correlated. If the points corresponding to pairs of values of x and y were plotted on a scatter diagram, they would lie on a straight line. If $r = +1$, the variables increase or decrease together. If $r = -1$, then as one increases, the other decreases. If $r = 0$, statistically there is no correlation. Values between 0 and 1 or 0 and -1 give a measure of the strength of the correlation which lies between none and complete. It is important to remember that the coefficient of correlation and other measures of relationship say nothing about cause and effect. They merely measure the strength of the relationship if one exists. Other evidence for its existence must be sought.

The statistical concepts which the numerate manager should keep in mind then are:

1 a choice of representative of the data;
2 a measure of reliability of the chosen representative;
3 making allowances for fluctuations in data and particularly regarding the operations of chance;
4 methods of establishing the strength of relationships and associations.

Aware of these aspects of processing data, he may leave the rest to his experts. An awareness of them will provide an environment in which good actions will result from the initial data. Good action, however, may be made better by efficiency in handling. Thought therefore needs to be given not only to the steps to be taken in order to proceed from data to action, but also to the manner in which they are taken.

CLASSIFICATION OF INFORMATION

An understanding of the fundamental nature of information and the manner in which it can be classified is a first necessity. Required to name a repository of information, most people would have very little difficulty in designating a library as the answer. Asked further if they were aware of how the information was classified and stored, most would again have little difficulty in describing how the information was broken down into various broad items, such as architecture, bee-keeping, carpentry, etc., the information relating to each item being collected together under its appropriate heading. The headings themselves would be arranged according to some convenient order, more often than not alphabetical. This is so much the familiar method of arranging information that one is apt to think of it as the natural way in which it should be done.

The library system of arranging information is certainly widely copied. In the business sphere it would be found in a set of personnel records, the items being the group of separate employees. The sales ledger is a collection of items, each of which represents an individual customer. In both cases the commonest order in which these items would be found is alphabetical, but an alternative not infrequently found is an arrangement by reference to a series of numerical account numbers or clock numbers. The broad items may themselves be broken down into a series of sub-items. Architecture might consist of the architecture of cathedrals, the architecture of small dwellings or public buildings. Each of these in turn may be broken down into further smaller items appertaining to the various eras— classical, mediaeval, Georgian and so on. Smaller classifications still might be, perhaps, by regions, such as English, French or Italian. However far the sub-divisions are taken, the same principles of grouping, classifying and ordering will be found.

This system of classification came into being to serve a particular purpose. This was that the store of information could be used efficiently to provide the answers to a particular type of question. The type of question most commonly asked was that relating to specific items. What is there known about bee-keeping? What tools are needed if one wants to take up carpentry? What use have English architects of public buildings made of Cotswold stone? Such were the kinds of questions, and the library system of classification enables the answers to be quickly found.

As the information tree shows, by selecting successive branches,

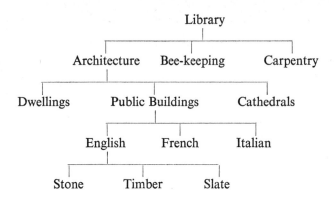

the route leading to the location of the information concerning the item being investigated is clearly marked. It points to the shelves in the library where the books on architecture are to be found; to the section devoted to public buildings; to a particular book describing English public buildings; to a particular chapter concerned with the use of stone; and to a particular paragraph in which Cotswold stone is discussed.

So it is with any system organized to answer primarily item questions. The search for information as to whether Tom Brown of the press shop can speak French goes first to the personnel department, then to the filing cabinet where the records are kept; to the press shop drawer; to Tom Brown's file and, finally, to an entry in that file listing the languages he speaks. Because the type of question most often asked in the past has been the question concerning an item, and because the library system of classification promotes efficiency in obtaining the answer, this system has come to be regarded as the natural way of classifying information, whatever the use to be made of it.

This is to ignore the fact that there is another type of question. This, not often asked in the past, is asked with increasing frequency in modern times. It relates to particular features of the information. The question 'What use have English architects of public buildings made of Cotswold stone?' relates to a very precise item. The item, however, is made up of several features:

The feature of architecture
The feature of public buildings
The feature of English

The feature of stone
The feature of Cotswold.

On the other hand, when enquiry is made concerning a feature itself, then the enquiry has to direct itself to all the places where something may be said about that feature. Thus, for instance, if 'stone' is being investigated it is necessary to find out about not only stone used by English architects, but also stone used by French architects and Italian architects and architects of every other nationality. Moreover, this stone as used by architects of every nationality may be used not only in public buildings, but also in dwelling houses and cathedrals and in every other sub-division of the topic of architecture. Finally, information concerning it is not confined to the shelves on architecture. It will appear under road-building, geology, ancient warfare, to name a few. Moreover, there is no way of knowing in advance, under the library system of classification, whether or not a particular feature will be included in any item. Every piece of information that is stored has to be inspected before it can be decided that it has nothing to say about the feature. There are of course ways of expediting the search. In a set of personnel records, one filing cabinet may contain male records and another female. If the feature being investigated is known to be exclusively male, then the filing cabinet containing the female records will not be opened. Nevertheless, they have in fact been considered and rapidly rejected as having nothing to contribute. The process has been fore-shortened to an inspection of the labels on the filing cabinets or a quick mental consultation of one's memory to recall where the male records are kept. But an inspection has nevertheless been mentally effected, leading to a clear decision to ignore all such items of one particular kind. It should be noticed that this is true whatever the method of storing the information.

In an electronic computer, the filing cabinet may be replaced by a reel of magnetic tape, and the label on the drawer by a particular electronic signal preceding the signals which represent the data. The computer programme must allow for a positive inspection of the first signal so that the following data can be accepted for further inspection or rejected. This principle applies whatever the method used to handle the data, whenever the system of classifying the data is the library item classification system. In every case, feature questions can only be answered by searches, some long, some short, through the whole of the data.

FEATURE QUESTIONS

In practice, throughout business both item questions and feature questions are posed for answering. In practice also, more often than not, the system of classification of data which obtains is the library type which, as has been seen, is better designed for answering item questions. If the majority of questions are item questions, then this is as it should be, but in modern times such questions are becoming relatively fewer and fewer. More and more feature questions are being asked. In information retrieval systems, the requirement is to find all that is known on a particular subject. This is a feature question which would involve, in an item classification system, a protracted search through the store of data. In the analysis of sales data, it is the comparison of a piece of information with other pieces of information, or the collating of many pieces of information, that requires to be done. These are feature questions. In personnel work, too, the requirement is as often to discover all the members of the staff who possess a particular feature, such as having completed forty years' service, as it is to discover facts confined to any single individual.

As the incidence of feature questions increases, it becomes desirable to see whether there are more suitable systems of classification. This can be found if the unit of record is taken to be a feature and not an item, and if the particulars recorded under the feature heading are taken to be references to those items which possess that feature. The index to any book is just that sort of classification designed to answer questions as to where information concerning particular features is located. An index is a rather simple feature classification. In such a restricted form it cannot easily be used to answer feature questions involving comparison and collation. To do so, a pattern of registration must be injected into the system.

Suppose a group of data consists of items 1, 2, 3, 4, 5, 6, 7, 8, 9 and 10, and features A, B, C, D, E, F and G. In an item classification, be it books on library shelves, files in a filing cabinet, a stack of punched cards or pages in a loose-leaf ledger, the form of the classification will be as follows:

	Items									
	1	2	3	4	5	6	7	8	9	10
Features	A	B	A	D	C	A	B	A	E	A
	D	C	B	G	E	C	D	D	F	G
	G	E	G		F	D	E	E	G	
		F			G	G	F	G		
		G								

This provides an easy means of discovering the make-up of each of the items. It is not quite such an easy means of comparing even one item with another, and an even less easy means of discovering how the features are distributed. The latter question is answered by the simple form of feature classification as in a book index. Thus:

			Features			
A	**B**	**C**	**D**	**E**	**F**	**G**
1	2	2	1	2	2	1
3	3	5	4	5	5	2
6	7	6	6	7	7	3
8			7	8	9	4
10			8	9		5
						6
						8
						9
						10

Items

In particular this shows clearly the wide distribution of feature *G*. It still does not, however, provide any easy means of making comparisons. To do so a pattern of arrangement is necessary as, for instance, the following:

			Features			
A	**B**	**C**	**D**	**E**	**F**	**G**
1			1			1
	2	2		2	2	2
3	3					3
			4			4
		5		5	5	5
6		6	6			6
	7		7	7	7	
8			8	8		8
				9	9	9
10						10

Items

Now it is easy to discern the answers to questions such as 'Where can one find the combination of features *A*, *D* and *G*?'—Answer, items 1, 6 and 8. 'Which of those items which possess features *A*, *D* and *G* also possesses *C*?'—Answer, item 6.

Patterned arrangement by feature enables feature questions to be answered by discerning coincidence. This is true even if the mechanism of recording is other than a manual listing of reference numbers. Punched cards, where each card represents some particular feature possessed by any of the items in the collection of data, are equally suitable. In the collection of data represented above there would be eight separate feature cards, *A, B, C, D, E, F* and *G*. The items in which a particular feature was found would be indicated by punching holes in appropriate positions on the card. Thus the card for the feature *A*, assuming allowance is made for twelve items, would be as in Figure 24, holes being punched in positions 1, 3, 6, 8 and 10, the remaining positions being left unpunched, and each feature card being punched in similar fashion.

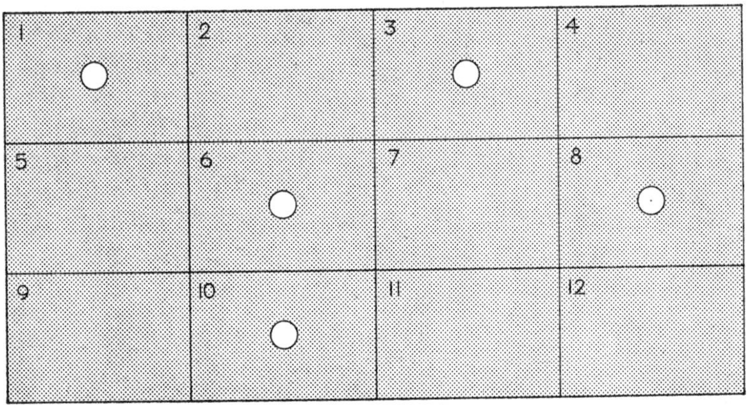

FIG. 24—Card for feature *A*.

To answer a feature question such as the one posed 'Where can one find the combination of features *A, D* and *G*?', all that is necessary is to select the three feature cards *A, D* and *G* and stack them. By noting where the holes coincide the question is answered.

The coincidence in a manual system can be discerned by inspection; in a mechanical system by pins which will go through all the cards with holes in the same positions. Similar arrangements in an electronic system make electrical contacts which initiate certain actions in consequence.

Whatever the means of handling the cards, if a feature system of classification is in use, no longer is it necessary to inspect all the data in order to answer feature type questions. Areas of business where feature-type questions are becoming common are retrieval systems used in conjunction with the storage of scientific and technical information, analysis of business data and the searching of administrative records.

As always, the requirement for the numerate manager is to be aware of the distinction that can be drawn in the types of questions for which answers are sought, to understand the principles of application and to accept the need for specifying requirements at an earlier stage of the decision-making process than before.

PROCESSES OF REASONING

The topics dealt with so far in this chapter have been concerned with the objectives of transforming data into information and with those characteristics of information which will affect the quality of the end product, the decision and the action based upon it. There are other characteristics of information which affect the efficiency of the reasoning process, and to these some thought must be given. Some of these reasoning processes have been considered in Chapter II, *Some Tools of Numeracy*. These were stylized processes applicable to the solution of certain formalized problems. Wider than these, and deeper than them, is the whole theory of thinking known as logic. If the decisions on which action is to be based are to be rational ones, then the processes by which they are reached must be rational also. This in turn requires some understanding of the nature of the processes and of what this involves in the way of specifying information.

Thinking itself may be of two kinds. It may be directed towards finding an immediate solution to a problem, or it may be concerned with extending a knowledge of truth which will colour directed thinking at a later date. A manager faced with a wage demand from his employees has to direct his thinking towards the decision he must make concerning it. He will also at other times, or even at the same time, contemplate the general economic situation and the psychology of trade union officials with a view to being better equipped to deal with similar problems in the future. In both types the thinking will be effective only so far as the data being considered is relevant to the problem under immediate consideration or to the knowledge sought. One of the methods by which the passage from data to conclusion is effected is by the process of inference. By inference one accepts a conclusion on the basis of the data considered as evidence. What is sought is that this evidence should be decisive. Even if there is some evidence in favour of the conclusion and none contrary, it does not follow that it is decisive. Evidence is decisive only when acceptance of the conclusion results of necessity from acceptance of the evidence. Inability to recognize evidence of this sort may come from ignorance, or it may arise because emotion takes the place of reason. The first can be avoided by education, the second by training.

Inference can be used to reach generalizations. From information that all women interviewed by a market research team chose blue, it may be inferred that a product coloured blue will appeal to all women. This may hold so long as no contrary evidence is discovered, but one single exception discovered will contradict a generalization. In this type of inference, known as inductive inference, the premisses which are the starting point of the inference may be true, yet the conclusion may be false. It can certainly be true that all the women interviewed chose blue, yet it can equally certainly be untrue that a product coloured blue will appeal to all women, whether they have been interviewed or not.

When one moves to deductive inference, however, the truth of the premisses automatically guarantees the truth of the conclusion. Consider this example of deductive inference:

> Premisses:　Only chlorophyll will make the colour of tooth-
> paste green.
> This toothpaste is green.
> Conclusion:　This toothpaste contains chlorophyll.

In the argument just described there are three statements which are known as propositions. The first two propositions entail the third. A fundamental logical principle can now be stated. 'Whatever is entailed by a true proposition is itself true.' This is the principle of deduction, and by it one is enabled validly to infer one proposition from another. Thus it is not permissible to accept a hypothesis and reject its consequences.

These principles are quite general and are not concerned with any particular data. They relate only to the form of the reasoning. It is important to realize that the logical conclusiveness of an argument depends upon its form and on nothing else. Not all reasoning is deductive, but all logically conclusive reasoning is deductive.

The bulk of business decision-making has tended to be based on inductive inference and if only 'good enough' decisions are being sought this will more often than not, suffice. The greater precision required for 'best' decisions, however, points to the desirability of extending methods of reasoning to include wherever possible deductive inference. This has its importance also when modern information systems are being devised.

If an information store contains the numerals 0, 1, 2, 3, 4, 5, 6, 7, 8, 9 as facts of an information system, it would be considered perfectly natural to refrain from storing the further 'facts' that $1,002+3,829 = 4,831$ or that $27 \times 98 = 2,646$ for example. These facts are capable of being deduced from the accepted axioms of mathematics.

Similarly, if the policy of a firm is to engage only men who are British subjects, it is an unnecessary use of time and information storage space to record on an employee's personnel record that the employee is male and is British. Given that the fact of the firm's policy and that the individual is a member of the firm are accepted as true and that the appropriate form of reasoning is accepted as valid, the further facts can be deduced rather than recorded. This principle can be extended to much more complicated situations and assumes a greater value when, as in modern electronic systems, information storage space becomes costly.

Deductive reasoning has a long history dating backwards to the fundamental work of Aristotle and manifesting itself in modern mathematical set theory. Some appreciation of the basic concepts used in deductive reasoning and of the purpose of the specialized language in which these concepts are expressed may not come amiss.

Various relationships can be distinguished between propositions. First, they may be incompatible—that is they cannot be true together. In this case of course the truth of one cannot be inferred from the truth of the other. However, when it is known that two propositions are incompatible, knowledge of the truth of one of them provides the basis of the inference that the other is false.

The opposite relationship to incompatibility is compatibility. Compatibility itself is too general a relationship to be useful. It is necessary to define rather more specific relationships within the framework of compatibility. One such is independence. Where this prevails, two propositions may be compatible but independent, and neither can afford a basis for inferring the other.

Another is equivalence. If two propositions are equivalent, then the truth or falsity of the second can be inferred from the truth or falsity of the first and vice versa. A pair of equivalent propositions is, for example, 'All dogs have four legs' and 'No dogs have not got four legs'. Or again the proposition 'If the Socialist Government proceeds with the nationalization of steel, then the Conservatives will oppose the Steel Bill' is equivalent to 'Either the Socialist

Government will not proceed with the nationalization of steel or the Conservatives will oppose the Steel Bill'.

It is not always the case that two propositions are exactly equivalent if one of them can be inferred from the other. It may not be permissible to infer the latter from the former. Thus, if the initial proposition is that 'All men wear trousers,' it is permissible to infer the proposition that 'Some men wear trousers,' but if the initial proposition is that 'Some men wear trousers' it is not permissible to infer that 'All men wear trousers'. The relationships here are known as (a) sub-implication, referring to the inference of the first proposition from the second, and (b) super-implication, defining the relationship of the second to the first.

One other relationship is known in logic as sub-contrary. Two propositions may both be true but cannot both be false. In such a case, if it is known that one proposition is false, then it can be inferred that the other is true, but if it is known that one is true then nothing can be inferred about the other.

FUNDAMENTAL PRINCIPLES OF LOGIC

Fundamental to applying logic are two principles. These can be stated as:

1 a proposition cannot be both true and false;
2 a proposition is either true or false.

The first is the principle of non-contradiction and the second is the principle of excluded middle. Caution must be used to ensure that these principles are applied only to those propositions where there is some significance in attaching a property to the object being discussed. There would be little point in applying the principle of non-contradiction to the pair of propositions 'Cowardice is egg-shaped' and 'Cowardice is not egg-shaped'.

There is a very important distinction to be drawn between a universal proposition and a particular proposition. Universal propositions are of the form 'All Xs are Ys' or 'No Xs are Ys', while a proposition that 'some Xs are Ys would be a particular proposition. Universal propositions and particular propositions may be compatible, but it is not permissible to infer a universal proposition from a particular proposition. In propositions of the form All, No or Some Xs are Ys, X is referred to as the subject and Y as the predicate. The subject or the predicate may be referred to as including every member of the class. If so, it is said to be distributed.

The principles of logic can be used to lay bare truth in a number of ways. One of the commonest forms of argument is to apply a general rule to a specified case in order to achieve some resulting conclusion. Such are known as syllogisms and these may take a number of shapes. To some of these, special names have been given, of which one of the most famous is Barbara. Its shape is:

> Every Y is Z
> Every X is Y
> Therefore every X is Z.

The first two statements are the premisses. The third is the conclusion. Thus, for example,

> 'Every Scotsman likes whisky
> Every company chairman is a Scotsman
> Therefore every company chairman likes whisky'.

is Barbara.

If the syllogism is being used in argument it is important to know the conditions in which it may be valid. Logicians have collected together these rules which, if they are obeyed, certify the validity of a syllogism:

1 the middle term must be distributed in at least one of the premisses;
2 if a term is distributed in the conclusion it must have been distributed in the corresponding premiss;
3 at least one premiss must be affirmative;
4 if one premiss is negative, the conclusion must be negative;
5 if both premisses are affirmative, the conclusion must be affirmative.

As in the quantified logic of mathematics, the language makes use of symbols. In stating the proposition 'all X are Y', the use of X and Y makes it a quite general statement, whether or not it is known what the X and Y represent. It is sometimes helpful to use S and P as symbols in stating the four possible forms found in traditional logic. These then become:

1 All S are P
2 No S are P
3 Some S are P
4 Some S are not P.

Propositions 1 and 3 are affirmative propositions, while 2 and 4 are in negative forms. The Latin for 'I affirm' is '*affirmo*', of which the first two vowels are *a* and *i*. Propositions 1 and 3 can be written in shortened form as $S a P$ and $S i P$ respectively. The Latin for 'I deny' is '*nego*' of which the first two vowels are *e* and *o*. Propositions 2 and 4 can be written in shortened form $S e P$ and $S o P$.

It is convenient to refer to the universal affirmative proposition $S a P$ as the *A proposition*, the universal negative proposition $S e P$ as the *E proposition*, the particular affirmative proposition $S i P$ as the *I proposition* and the particular negative proposition $S o P$ as the *O proposition*.

The advantage of using symbolic language of this sort is that the general principles of argument can be tested without relation to the truth or falsity of statements when the symbols have specific meanings. In this, logic follows a course parallel to the development of algebra, and other forms of mathematical analysis, where the validity of arguments can be established by pure reasoning and their application to specific cases handled after it is known that it is legitimate to do so.

In handling information, particularly in business operations, a single piece of information is rarely handled in isolation. It is its position as part of a set of information that is of interest. The concept of sets has already been met in considering the methods of classifying information. A library can be considered as a set, broken down into subsets, each of which in turn may consist of further subsets. A company is a set of resources—machines, personnel, materials, etc. Each of these can be broken down further into subsets. Personnel, for instance, will be of different kinds—clerical, managerial, craftsmen, operating and so on. In order to add precision to discussions involving sets, a symbolic language is needed, of which the principal concepts can be summarized as follows:

A set S has to be considered both as an entity of its own and as a collection of its separate items. Thus the members of the population who buy baked beans may be designated as the set B, while the set of odd integers may be designated $(1, 3, 5, 7, \ldots \ldots)$. If there are five manufacturers of baked beans, P, Q, R, S and T, and each purchaser of baked beans is completely loyal to one manufacturer, then the set B could be designated (p, q, r, s, t), where p stands for those people who buy P's baked beans, q those who buy Q's baked beans and so on. In this latter set there is a limit to the number of the elements in the set, while in the set of odd integers there is no limit to it. The set of baked beans purchasers is therefore a finite set, while the set of odd integers is an infinite set.

It may be that the purchasers of baked beans are not loyal to one manufacturer. Those who sometimes buy P's baked beans and sometimes Q's are designated pq. Suppose there are three manufacturers. It is possible to designate in this way:

$$(p)\ (q)\ (r)\ (pq)\ (pr)\ (qr)\ (pqr)$$

It will be noticed that the letters and combinations of letters have been enclosed within the sign denoting the composition of a set and each of them does comprise a set. These seven sets are subsets of the set B. For completeness, an eighth subset should be designated, consisting of those purchasers of baked beans who cannot be identified with either p, q or r. In this case it is an empty set because all members of B are identified, and it is denoted by the Greek letter ϕ which stands for a null set.

It is important information that an element x belongs to a set A. This is written as $x \in A$. For example, *Mrs. Brown* $\in p$ means that Mrs Brown buys P's baked beans and only P's baked beans.

A subset X of another set Y means that every element in X is also an element of Y. It is designated as $X \subseteq Y$. If the two sets S and T contain the same elements and only the same elements then they are said to be identical and $S = T$. It follows that $S \subseteq T$ and $T \subseteq S$. Thus, if P has an absolute monopoly of the baked beans market, then $p \subseteq B$ and $B \subseteq p$. The significance of this is that, when it is known that this relationship exists, p can be identified by investigating B. Information concerning B may be more easily found in particular cases, possibly indirectly, if it is known that all who are not members of some other class C, the purchasers of spaghetti, for instance, are members of B.

The identification of elements which are not members of a set is as important as the identification of elements which are members. If s denotes the members of set S, then another set can be identified consisting of elements which are not members of S. This is denoted by S' or $\bar{S}$. In the example considered B is the set comprising all the purchasers of baked beans, and p those who purchase baked beans manufactured by P. If p' is defined as those members of the population who purchase baked beans but not those manufactured by P, then $B = p + p'$ and $p' = B - p$. Care needs to be taken in

M

formulating the definition of the sets, since it is possible to form another set p' which includes not only those members of the population who purchase baked beans not manufactured by P, but also those members of the population who do not purchase any baked beans at all.

In order to develop a theory of sets, it is necessary to provide descriptions of certain combinations. Thus the union of two sets X and Y comprises the set of items belonging to X or Y or both. This is denoted by $X \cup Y$. Another combination frequently met is the set of items belonging to both X and Y. This, the intersection of X and Y, is denoted by $X \cap Y$. Thus, suppose X is the set of people who buy a product P represented by p, as well as those who buy Q represented by q, there being none who buy both, $X = (p, q)$. Similarly $Y = (p, r)$, r being those who buy product R. Then $X \cup Y = (p, q, r)$, while $X \cap Y = (p)$.

It can be shown that the following properties of set operations hold:

$$X \cup (Y \cup Z) = (X \cup Y) \cup Z$$
$$X \cap (Y \cap Z) = (X \cap Y) \cap Z$$
$$X \cup Y = Y \cup X$$
$$X \cap Y = Y \cap X$$
$$X \cup (Y \cap Z) = (X \cup Y) \cap (X \cup Z)$$
$$X \cap (Y \cup Z) = (X \cap Y) \cup (X \cap Z)$$

To the uninitiated, for whom the form of language is strange, such definitions and operations can be mystifying. Yet the concepts they describe are straightforward and, when recast in more familiar language, are easy to follow. The following example can be used to illustrate them.

Suppose market research establishes preferences for three products X, Y and Z amongst a sample of 500 males.

	X	Y	Z
Males	120	70	220

If A is the set of males, then A has 500 members.

If S is the set of males who prefer one of the three products, then

$$S = 120 + 70 + 220 = 410$$

and
$$S' = A - S = 500 - 410 = 90$$

If P is the set of males who prefer X
Q is the set of males who prefer Y
R is the set of males who prefer Z, then

$P \cup Q$ is the set of males who prefer X or Y and it has 190 members

$Q \cup R$ is the set of males who prefer Y or Z and it has 290 members

$$(P \cup Q) \cup R = 190 + 220 = 410$$
$$P \cup (Q \cup R) = 120 + 290 = 410$$

Hence

$$(P \cup Q) \cup R = P \cup (Q \cup R)$$

as required. Similarly the truth of the other operations can be found in terms of the value shown.

Stated thus the rules are simple, and indeed trivial. The justification for stating them in formal language is that they then provide fixed guide-lines in situations where conclusions are not so obvious, and can also be used to develop more sophisticated relationships which lead to more profound conclusions.

A visual aid in discussing the operations of sets is due to the British logician John Venn, and hence is known as a Venn diagram.

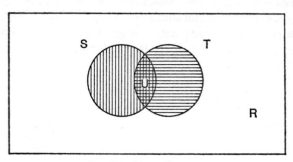

FIG. 25.—Venn diagram.

Consider a universe R which comprises all the members under investigation. This is denoted by the rectangle R. Two subsets S and T of the whole set R are represented by the two circles.

$S \cup T$ is the total shaded area.
$S \cap T$ is the cross-hatched area (U).
$(S \cup T)'$ is the unshaded area.

The other fundamental relationships can be easily discovered.

All sales analysis work deals with sets. The different groupings of a population, each of which has particular tastes or combinations of tastes, can be illustrated in terms of sets and subsets and vice versa. The logical rules defined are a means of keeping a clear head when the groupings become numerous or complex.

The handling of information within an organization does not take place in a vacuum. It must be provided with an environment and the nature of the environment provided has an important influence on the meaning that is distilled from the information and on the quality of the decisions that emerge from the distilled meaning. Numeracy requires on the part of a manager, in addition to his awareness of the nature of the problems he has to solve, his ability to understand the language in which problems are effectively solved and the kind of approach which leads to the solution he seeks, and also a keen sense of the organizational structure that is necessary to administer the problem-solving groups. He must be clear as to his position in the structure. The conventional form of structure of the past has been the pyramid designed to support the manager at the top. This, however, puts too much emphasis on the struts necessary to provide strength upwards, and too little on the struts necessary to provide strength laterally and downwards. Managers have been following a road which has been well mapped out over recent years. That road still stretches out into the future, but another road can now be discerned, and managers have a choice to make as to which to follow. The manager is at the cross-roads.

CHAPTER VI

MANAGER AT THE CROSS-ROADS

PROFESSIONALISM IN MANAGEMENT

MACAULAY, in his essay on Francis Bacon, has this to say of Sir Nicholas Bacon, Chancellor of England during the first twenty years of the reign of Elizabeth I, and the father of Francis: 'He belonged to a set of men whom it is easier to describe collectively than separately, whose minds were formed by one system of discipline, who belonged to one rank in society, to one university, to one party, to one sect, to one administration, and who resembled each other so much in talents, in opinions, in habits, in fortunes, that one character, we had almost said one life, may to a considerable extent, serve for them all.'

The population of England has been estimated to have been just over four million in the time of Elizabeth. This is approximately the number of those shown by official statistics to have been employed in 1966 in the gas, electricity and water undertakings, and slightly less than those employed in that same year in the chemical and allied industries. The statesmen of the Elizabethan age were the businessmen of the day and the scale of their activities was the equivalent of a major industry in modern times. Of more significance was the rapid expansion of activity that was taking place. In his *English Social History*, Professor G. M. Trevelyan gave his view that the population of London, for instance, doubled during the reign of Elizabeth. Those were pre-mechanization days and, since work was performed manually, the expansion in population gives a measure of the pace of development in the business of the country.

Macaulay, in the essay previously quoted, goes on to describe what this rapid expansion meant in terms of the evolution of statecraft or management, as it would be termed today. He writes of Nicholas Bacon and his followers: 'They were the first generation of statesmen by profession that England produced. Before their time the division of labour had, in this respect, been very imperfect. Those who had directed public affairs had been, with few exceptions, warriors or priests; warriors whose rude courage was neither guided by science nor softened by humanity, priests whose learning and abilities were habitually devoted to the defence of tyranny and imposture.' After discussing briefly the characteristics of the previous managers of the realm, Macaulay goes on: 'But the increase of wealth, the progress of knowledge, and the reformation of religion produced a great change. The nobles ceased to be military chieftains; the priests ceased to possess a monopoly of learning; and a new and remarkable series of politicians appeared.

'These men came from neither of the classes which had, till then, almost exclusively furnished ministers of state. They were all laymen; yet they were all men of learning; and they were all men of peace. They were not members of the aristocracy. They inherited no titles, no large domains, no armies of retainers, no fortified castles. Yet they were not low men, such as those whom princes, jealous of the power of a nobility, have sometimes raised from forges and cobblers' stalls to the highest situations. They were all gentlemen by birth. They had all received a liberal education.'

The parallel between the situation Macaulay was describing and that existing today can be discerned. Again a new race of managers is emerging with its own characteristics and its own form of expertise. Mr Fred Catherwood, Director-General of the National Economic Development Office, and others have drawn attention to the professionalism which is their objective and which requires to be more widely spread, as they claim, if progress is to be continued and accelerated. The managers of any era, however, have always possessed a professionalism. It has been the professionalism appropriate to its age. It is not the emergence of a professionalism that is significant, but the change in its nature. Those who are now being superseded are not the direct descendants of Elizabethan statesmen. The latter, or their immediate descendants, found it impossible to keep in the same hands the conduct of the affairs of state and the direction of the growing commercial and industrial enterprises. Forced to choose, they chose to operate on the national and political scale, leaving no others whom they considered as their inferiors the lesser activities.

In these spheres, which had thus become separated from national and political organizations, the first industrial revolution took root and flowered. Its effect was precisely the same as had occurred in Elizabethan times. Again a new group of professionals emerged with their own new expertise and their own new attributes, including now that of literacy, an attribute which had hitherto been confined to those operating on the national scale. The area of application changed over the years. Starting with a need to get things done and requiring a willingness to take one's coat off and get on with things, it moved on to a knowledge of methods of financing and an ability to obtain the means of making the wheels of industry turn. This change can be seen quite clearly reflected in the relatively high rewards which came to be paid to qualified accountants and others of a financial background in the first half of the twentieth century. Today, the important expertise required is directed to discovering what to do instead of how to implement what has already been decided. Hence the emergence of a new breed of managers more and more concerned with decision-making.

THE ATTRIBUTE OF NUMERACY

The professionalism has changed its nature and a new attribute is necessary for the manager who would aspire to be a professional decision-maker. This is the attribute of numeracy, as it has been defined in the preceding chapters. Its requirements may be summarized as follows:

1 taking a comprehensive view of problem-solving involving an open-minded approach to knowledge wherever it may be found;
2 a willingness to examine every problem in considerable detail involving the identification of every element in the situation being examined;
3 tracing the inter-relationships between each and every element;
4 measuring in the unit appropriate to the problem the value of each element and the strength of every force affecting it;
5 using the most powerful suitable deductive techniques regardless of the branch of knowledge from which they originate;
6 having the courage to accept the conclusions.

This is the antithesis of intuitive decision-making and is in effect conceptual model-building, in contrast to physical model-building on the basis of a hunch. Practised successfully, it brings very real advantages in the shape of reductions in the cost of achieving successful decisions, as well as a much more complete understanding of all the problems being tackled. It can also bring spectacular failures if the conditions for building conceptual models are not right. Ensuring that the conditions are right is a managerial responsibility.

The climate in which the problem is set must be understood. This climate may be a deterministic one in which one result follows inexorably from one or more causes. Thus sales of a product at a fixed price for cash result in a certain amount of money in the till, determined by the quantity of the product sold and its price. It may, on the other hand, be a stochastic climate in which, although a pattern of events exists, variations occur within that pattern. Thus, doubling the advertising appropriation can be expected, in general and over a period, to produce a given increase in sales, but within that general pattern there will be fluctuations in the amount of the increase over various areas and at different times.

For example, it is stated that $4\frac{1}{2}$ ounces of potatoes and $\frac{1}{2}$ ounce of vegetable oil will produce half an ounce of potato crisps. The precise quantity of potato crisps will fluctuate round that value for successive batches, although a year's production will throw up that value accurately. Probably the climate of business situations is rather more often stochastic than deterministic, although decision-making processes in the past have either assumed that they are always deterministic or have made no precise allowances for their stochastic nature. Finally, the climate may be an entirely random one where no causal relationships can be established. Entirely random situations are comparatively rare. There are many either deterministic or stochastic situations or a mixture of the two in which randomness also plays a part, however. Thus, a petrol station situated near a factory will have a pattern of custom which will have a deterministic, a stochastic and a random part to it. Credit arrangements made with certain customers will provide the deterministic part. The times at which the factory starts and stops work will provide the stochastic part. Customers unconnected with the regular clientele or the factory will provide the random part.

Defining the boundaries of the problem is also a managerial duty. It is the manager who must decide what, if any, restrictions are to be placed on possible solutions. He it is who must decide the relative importance to be attached to various pieces of information. He it is who must take the responsibility if, for the sake of simplifying the issues, certain areas of the problem are to be eliminated from consideration. Above all, he must clearly state what is the objective to be aimed at and what is the criterion by which the merit of a solution is to be judged.

As with any other form of decision-making which takes account of facts, the quality of the measurements which express the facts

influences the quality of the decision. Factors affecting the quality
of the measurements are:

1 the choice of the units appropriate to the problem;
2 the method by which the measurements are made;
3 the degree of accuracy required in the measurements.

Although not himself actively engaged in the process of making
the measurements, the manager cannot absolve himself from the
responsibility for them. He must accept it and he must either make
the decisions concerning the factors mentioned or he must accept
decisions made on his behalf.

Neither can the manager divest himself of the responsibility for
choosing the right method of solving any particular problem. Right
at the start he must decide to which problem-solving group it
should be sent, and whether it requires a numerate or non-numerate
approach. He must, too, at the very least by implication, accept
responsibility for the choice of technique that is used to ·solve the
problem.

The manager has his experts to assist him in implementing his
responsibilities. They do not relieve him of his duties. What they
do take from him, once he has carried out his duties of definition
and specification, is the actual process of reaching the decision.
Herein lies the difference from former practice. When the process
is complete, the manager is required to accept or reject it. Strictly
speaking, he is not entitled to modify it. In practice, of course, he
may have second thoughts regarding the nature of the problem
and its specification. In fact, when he does this he is posing a new
problem, having abandoned the first, and should go through the
same procedure as before to find its solution. The manager has
final powers and may elect not to do so. This is his privilege, but in
exercising it he must be clear in his own mind that the method of
reaching the solution he is now adopting is not a rational one.
He ought also to be clear that he can justify, even if only to himself,
his use of an irrational method.

This withdrawal from the process of reaching the decision is
seen clearly enough when a computer is in use to do the processing.
The use of the computer is incidental and does not create the point
at issue. This arises from the use of a numerate method of decision-
making. It would be true if the method relied on clerical means of
processing the data. It is easier for the manager to accept the change
if a computer is in use, because he is unable to intervene. When a

computer is not in use he is physically able to intervene, but must discipline himself not to do so. Failure to discipline himself in this way prevents him from becoming truly numerate.

QUALITIES OF A NUMERATE MANAGER

The requirements of numeracy relative to the method of decision-making have now been listed and considered. The attribute of numeracy in relation to the make-up of the manager also needs consideration. The concept is too new to have generated any literature to date. Indeed the word does not appear in the Oxford Dictionary.

The published references to 'numeracy' have been slight and have not developed the concept. They have appeared to the author to have given a too restricted view of the attribute and to have confused it with being good at arithmetic. Dr J. M. S. Risk, commenting in *The Chartered Secretary* of May, 1966, wrote 'At the Eastbourne Conference in June, 1965, Sir Edward Playfair, K.C.B., claimed that managers required both literacy and "numeracy". To be handy with figures may be another way of expressing the same need.'

'To be handy with figures' is not, in the view of the author, synonymous with 'being numerate'. Numeracy is a far wider concept and, although it involves an appreciation of the value of figures and an understanding of the ways in which they can be used, its possessor need not himself be at all handy with figures. Nor is one who is handy with figures automatically numerate, even if he is an expert mathematician or a skilled scientist. If his outlook is localized and he is unable to create conceptual models on the widest possible base where necessary, he is non-numerate.

Numeracy involves for its possessor, certainly, sufficient familiarity with the specialized language of mathematics and logic that the implications of the techniques used can be understood and that the value of the results can be assessed. He must be able to decide whether the solution to one problem has any bearing on the solution of other problems also under consideration. He will have presented to him arguments from many sources whose soundness he desires to judge and from all of which he has to pick his final conclusions. Being numerate, he will know that his salvation does not in general lie in dividing up his problems into smaller sections in the hope that individually they will be easier to solve, because he will know that

by so doing he may eliminate some essential and important relationship. In consequence, the nature of the problem he is examining
changes and he runs the risk of getting an answer to a question he
had not intended to ask.

The numerate manager is concerned with the elements of a
problem only as elements, and must consider them completely
objectively. The expert who handles personnel matters, for instance,
will certainly have to rely in part on subjective judgements for his
assessment of the contribution made by the personnel element, and
of the effect the situation has in his own particular sphere. The
decision-maker, on the other hand, who has to take into account
the effect of all the other elements as well as personnel, needs to
know, and should be concerned only with, the expert's final assessment and his estimate of the probability of the assessment being
right. The decision-maker is in no position to alter the assessment,
since he himself is not an expert in any particular field. He may
have been an expert at some time in the past in one field or another,
but he is no longer a practising expert. He must avoid interfering
with the current expert's assessment. What he is entitled to do is
to require an explanation of the method by which the assessment
was made, and a justification of the probability of correctness that
the expert places upon it. This latter he is entitled to adjust, in the
light of his own opinions on the soundness of the methods used,
and he may too, if he thinks fit, return the assessment for revision.
To do more than that would be to usurp the function of the expert
who, by definition, has been appointed as the best man available
to prepare the assessment.

It is then the decision-maker's task to combine the individual
assessments, taking account of the relative importance he assigns to
each of them and of the inter-relationships between them and
external environmental elements known to him but not to the
experts. This process finally leads him to his decision, and it is to
enable him to do this successfully that he needs the attribute of
numeracy.

It is worth repeating that he does not need to be numerate if
either

1 he is not looking for the *best* solution but is satisfied with a
  good solution, i.e. *any* solution which provides him with an
  approved measure of efficiency; in such a case he is not concerned that he might have done better; or

2 the problem is a very localized one in which the elements are few in number, have no inter-relationships and are isolated from all external influences.

He may still find it useful, even in those circumstances, to be 'handy with figures'. This, however, as defined in this book, makes him merely a 'figurate' manager and not a 'numerate' one. Figuracy is concerned with the evaluation of courses of action when by some, usually arbitrary, method the whole range of possible courses of action has been narrowed down to a manageable few. Numeracy does not eliminate any courses of action in advance of consideration. Their elimination must be by a purely logical method. It chooses from the entire range of possibles. It is concerned with relative evaluation, and figurate methods may indeed later be needed to provide the exact evaluation once the choice has been made.

The evolution of industrial organizational structures is towards larger and larger units. Currently the fields of operation of these units become less and less simple as diversification in industry grows. In addition, relationships and interactions increase in number and complexity as operations become first nation-wide and then international. It would be surprising if these movements did not provide pressures on the methods of decision-making to cause them to take up also more comprehensive and more complex forms. It would be equally surprising if the changes in the methods of decision-making did not require the acquisition of new attributes by managers.

Numerate decision-making is akin to the function of the judge in a court of law. The judge cannot be knowledgeable in all the subjects he must consider. Specialized evidence is provided by witnesses who are expert in their own fields. What the judge is required to do is to ensure that the evidence is supplied in a way which will lead to the truth, not only of the individual piece of evidence but of its significance to the problem as a whole. Then he must see to it that all sides of the question are explored, making sure that the conduct of the case works to this end and that none of it transgresses the rules of legal decision-making. Finally he must, himself or through the agency of a jury, lead the case to a right conclusion by the exercise of proper deductive techniques. The more effective will he be in this, the more he eschews oratory and confines himself to cool objective analysis.

This is also the task of the numerate decision-maker, and it is as specialized a task as that of the judge. It requires an expert's knowledge of the methods of arriving at decisions, which has here been called numeracy, and it requires an involvement in the specifications of the information which is to be the raw material of the decisions.

ORGANIZATION OF INFORMATION FLOW

Information for decision-making in a business organization is required from three sources—environmental information of elements external to the organization, internal information of activities within the organization and information concerning interactions between the various decision-making areas. The structure of an information system is shown in Figure 26.

The decision-making areas are shown as spheres operating in the 'corridor of decision', each in contact with its neighbours. For smooth working there must be information flow between the spheres, acting as an oil to reduce the possible friction. Other information must flow in order to irrigate the decision-making areas

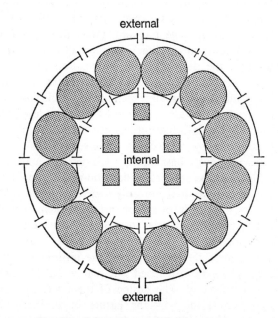

FIG. 26.—Information and decision-making.

so as to obviate sterile thinking. The corridor is separated from the area of internal activity by a porous membrane through which passes information concerning that activity. Similarly, a porous membrane separates the corridor from the external world, and through this passes the environmental information. If no restrictions are placed upon the flow through the two membranes, the only ultimate result must be the flooding of the corridor and consequent malfunctioning of the decision-making spheres. It is necessary, therefore, for filters to be designed to ensure that the flow is restricted to what is necessary for the decision-making. Within and without the corridor, the information flow is created by pumps situated in the various areas where activity is taking place. The design of the pumps and the design of the filters is all-important. The design of the pumps in the interior of the organization, and the design of the filters on both the interior and exterior membranes, is within the control of members of the organization. The design of the external pumps is in the hands of people who are not members of the organization.

Not a great deal of thought has, until recent years, been given to the choice of designer for these pieces of metaphorical equipment. Customarily, the structure of organizations has been such that in each internal area of activity the operators of the information pump located there have, in large measure, taken decisions concerning both the pump itself and the filter incorporated in it. In the case of external activity, the design of the information pumps is in the hands of persons not belonging to the organization, while the design of the filter has usually been in the hands of somebody specially assigned to the task, but at lower than top level. Hence the nature of the flow of information has not been determined, except in very broad terms, by the decision-makers themselves.

Such a structure has a basic fault, if the decision-making is to be numerate. Since all the spheres of decision-making in the corridor require to take into account not only their own local matters, but the influence of matters in other spheres upon their own also, it is necessary that they should have some say in the information that is to reach them. The design of the pump in the system must take into account principally the nature of the information that is to flow and can properly be carried out within the area where the information is generated. The design of the filter, however, must take into account principally the nature of the areas that the information flow is to irrigate. If it is carried out without reference to the experts in those areas, the risk may be high that the outflow through the filters may be unsuitable. If it is carried out by providing a series of individual designs for each of the spheres, the risk may be high that either one filter of such little inhibiting power is provided that it is hardly a filter at all, or that too many separate filters will be provided, several of which are redundant. It is essential therefore that the designing of the filtering processes should be handled at the decision-making level itself.

A step towards accepting this as a principle is now being taken on an increasing scale. This is to provide a management services department reporting to one or other of those within the decision-making corridor. However, if the reporting is to a member of the decision-making corridor who also controls an information-generating area of his own, there still exists a risk of bias in the filtering system and of a lack of awareness of the needs of all those who are going to contribute to the decision-making.

This bias can be avoided by one of three means:

1 the reporting can be to the managing director who takes responsibility for the design of the filtering system;
2 the management services group is headed by a director without other responsibilities;
3 the design of the filtering systems is accepted as a policy-making responsibility.

If none of these three courses is followed, the decision-making is being carried out with less than complete control over the raw material, namely information, that is used in the process. Less than complete control over the raw material in such an important process leads to less than the best end-product, namely the decision. By definition, the numerate manager seeks the best decision and therefore must ensure that control over information is complete.

Reference has already been made to the two distinct functions of management—leadership and decision-making. Of these two, leadership is concerned with the management of men, and decision-making with the management of information. In the former case the elements concerned are varied in their specific characteristics but stable in respect of changes over a period of time. Knowledge of the nature of the characteristics increases slowly over the years, but new techniques do not need to be developed suddenly to deal with new characteristics that have emerged in a short space of time. Well-tried techniques which have proved successful in the field of man management can continue with only gradual modification and occasional additions as new knowledge is acquired.

It is a very different situation as far as the management of information is concerned. Here the discovery of new characteristics of information and new forms of information is rapid. New knowledge to handle these also rapidly emerges, and this consists of entirely new forms of the decision-making process itself. To hold that the forms of decision-making have undergone little change over a long period requires either that the environment in ·which decision-making operates has remained unchanged, or that the decision-maker has acquired sufficient knowledge to support his intuitive judgement, or that he does not need the knowledge to support his intuition. It can hardly be argued that the world of business is the same as it was fifty years ago, far less as it was in Stonehenge times. The quantity of information and facts facing the decision-maker of today is vast, and increasing so rapidly that in his life span he could not hope to make it all his own. The experience needed to guide him in being selective could only come from that comprehensive knowledge which he has no longer time to acquire. A belief that knowledge is not required for decision-making is denied by the host of specialists now established and acquiring deep expertise in particular fields. A real dilemma now arises. The specialists are appointed because the decision-maker is unable to acquire the knowledge necessary to support his decision, yet finally it is the decision-maker who must make the decision. This requires judgement of some sort. Judgement based on an experience which is no longer relevant and on information and decision-making processes which are out of date will not do. It must be judgement based on the stable elements in a decision-making situation. The most stable element in such situations is the human brain and the power it possesses of reasoning. Knowledge of the methods and rules of reasoning can provide a stable base for judgement. The knowledge can be extended as more information concerning the processes of reasoning is made available through research and learning. The foundation of reasoning, however, does not suffer radical and revolutionary change.

The modern decision-maker is in a position, as has been said, akin to the judge in a court of law. Paraded before the judge is evidence on matters of fact or opinion; some of it is simple, but little is of a nature of which the judge has direct personal experience. The judge must control the argument according to formal rules designed to lead towards the emergence of truth in a particular form. This must be done objectively. The judge uses his best endeavours to see that subjective influences are ruled out. By the use of the processes of reasoning, either exercised personally or through direction to a jury, the decision is reached. So it is with the decision-maker, who sees to it that the specialist knowledge paraded before him is examined objectively, and that true judgements as to its reliability and importance are formed. By the process of reasoning the various strands are woven into a decision. Just as the judge requires his own specialist knowledge in the field of law to enable him to carry out his duty, so the decision-maker requires his own professional attribute, which in this book has been named numeracy.

THE PLACE OF THE DECISION-MAKER

Decision-making as so described is a very different activity from the exercise of leadership. Yet hitherto it has largely been assumed that ability in both directions can reside in one and the same person. When decision-making consisted of recognizing situations, reacting quickly to them and selecting one from a limited number of courses of action which had proved successful in the past and of which any was assumed to be good, this was true up to the necessary point. Decision-making today, however, is itself so specialized an activity, requiring additional attributes on the part of its practitioners, that it may not now be true. The movement towards greater and greater specializations is not one which is resisted in other affairs. It would therefore seem natural that the practice of management should lead to a separation of its functions. Its execution now seems likely to require both a leader and a decision-maker exercising these functions separately. The leader, in his capacity as an expert in the handling of men, has his contribution to make to the decision-making process, but his is not the responsibility for taking the decision. Nor is its execution the responsibility of the decision-maker. That responsibility lies with the leader.

The concept is not new. Plato envisaged it in his creation of guardians in his ideal state. In the modern British state, decision-making largely rests with the permanent civil servants or with part-time advisers, leadership being exercised by the government of the day. The armed forces have their separate staffs and field leaders. In business circles, the adviser behind the scenes, ostensibly merely

N

advising but quite often the real decision-maker, is not unknown. The use of outside consultants who are neutral and objective has increased greatly in recent years. In theory, a board of directors is a joint decision-making group, leadership being left to be carried out as a separate function by the managing director. What would be new at top level would be for formal recognition that these were two distinct functions, not to be combined in the one person but nevertheless to be performed within the organization.

This would mean a departure from the present pyramidical organizational structure and its replacement, for decision-making purposes, by groups or committees with the decision-maker as chairman. The constitution of the committees could vary according to the subject matter for which a decision was required, but the permanent chairman for each would require to be the permanent decision-maker chosen solely for his ability as a decision-maker. Lower levels of committees would have their own junior decision-makers as chairmen. This would form the hierarchy of decision-makers. Such an organization would then consist of:

1 the hierarchy of leaders in the conventional pyramid form;
2 the led, forming the base of the leadership pyramid;
3 the experts, providing the raw material for the decisions and processing this material;
4 the decision-makers, exercising their expertise in forming judgements.

These are four distinct groups, although the ranks of the leaders would often be fed from amongst those of the led. The other two groups, the experts and the decision-makers, would be self-contained groups, with, in general, no movement within the organization into or out of them. This is already the case with the group of experts as far as movement into the group is concerned. Except in the case of Imperial Chemical Industries Ltd., it is still normally the case that advancement to the top requires movement out of the group. The recent example set by ICI of making it possible for their experts to build a career within their scientific department equally advantageous to that possible in the spheres of 'management' is designed to make the best possible use of expertise.

The general application of this principle to cover experts throughout industry and commerce would prevent the waste of scarce knowledge, often fully acquired by the experts in time, merely to be left unused, as they move to other more general managerial duties which do not need it. The fourth group needs to be considered in the same light as being experts in decision-making. Their recruitment would be direct to the group, as in the case of other experts, scientific or professional. Thus the choice of this line to follow would have to be an early one, just as now the choice to become a doctor or a lawyer or a chemist is an early one. The pre-career training would be that appropriate to the acquiring of skills in the art of reasoning. This traditionally has involved the study of the classics and of philosophy and logic, and it might well be that a revival of these subjects is necessary for the decision-makers. In addition, however, the techniques of mathematical analysis and of measurement are necessary, while backing all these skills there needs to be provided as broad a knowledge as possible of current affairs, and economic and political movements. What does not seem to be necessary is any detailed knowledge of actual operations 'on the job'. This is for three reasons:

1 acquiring partial knowledge may prevent a truly objective assessment of all facts;
2 such knowledge in a period of rapid change becomes out of date;
3 such knowledge is best left to the experts.

The training of the decision-makers during their career might be along two lines. Initially they would spend a period of, say, one year in a junior operational job at the receiving end of instructions. This would provide knowledge of reactions and attitudes of thought on the part of those in that position. Further knowledge would come from attendance at courses, if necessary, in the subjects of economics and operational research and the methods of logical thought, such as are provided in the training of legal experts, i.e. the weighing of evidence, formal argument and the study of case law from the point of view of comprehending how evidence is sifted and made to lead to decisions. The development of the young decision-makers would be in the practice of decision-making. To this end they would act as chairmen, initially, of junior groups or committees, where the consequences of decisions taken are not of very great importance, but where nevertheless the arts of argument and the weighing of evidence can be practised.

If these contentions be accepted, the conventional form of 'on the job' and 'up the ladder' training needs to give way to a specialized 'on the job of decision-making' training for those who have opted and been chosen to join that specialized group. This is, of course, the civil service system, where entry is direct into the administrative class and experience is gained on more and more responsible decision-making, but always on decision-making. What is perhaps at fault in that system is the concentration of decision-making in too narrow a field with insufficient breadth of information to work upon. By contrast, the general position in the industrial and commercial scene is that the broad approach is there, but the need for skill in exercising the powers of reasoning is often decried, ignored or insufficiently acquired. There are signs that both these groups recognize the weaknesses and are taking steps to remedy them. Numeracy consists of the combination of the two approaches.

That the environment in which life is lived alters through the ages will not be disputed. That the practices of men in every sphere change too through the ages will be accepted. It would be strange if the practice of management alone did not change.

Change in the practice of management in a changing world is surely inevitable. Nevertheless, it should not be expected that change comes easily. It never has been so. In that same 'Essay on Bacon' from which the quotation came which opened this chapter, Macaulay comments on the way change comes about in the context of ideas on the management of Bacon's day and earlier: 'Opinions were still in a state of chaotic anarchy intermingling, separating, advancing, receding. Sometimes the stubborn bigotry of the Conservatives seemed likely to prevail. Then the impetuous onset of the Reformers for a movement carried all before it. Then again the resisting mass made a desperate stand, arrested the movement and forced it slowly back. The vacillation which at that time appeared in English legislation, and which it has been the fashion to attribute to the caprice and to the power of one or two individuals was truly a national vacillation.' But history shows that in the end change prevails.

Evolution brings about gradual modifications to practices, but periodically the great movements in history create a need for change rather than evolution. One such movement is the current second industrial revolution. Its effect is being seen on the practice of decision-making. Ultimately the change to the new type of decision-making will be complete. Management, as always, will adapt itself to the results of the change and managers will acquire the necessary new attribute of numeracy. In due course the educated will consider it as natural to be numerate as it is to be literate. The movement in this direction has begun, for in the schools already by 1966 some parts of the techniques and attitudes described in this book were being taught. By the end of the twentieth century there will be no problem. In the meantime, the existing managers will need to rely on their own efforts to provide themselves with the attribute of numeracy, in the realization that in the field of decision-making there will be no place for any but the numerate manager.

PROBABILITY AND
WAITING TIME PROBLEMS

A METHOD of developing a conceptual model for use in certain waiting time problems requires the state of the system under examination to be defined, and the changes that can occur in it to be investigated. When the probabilities of arrivals to the system, and of the completion of service to a unit in the system, can be expressed as simple mathematical functions, then practical formulae for the solution of problems involving the system can sometimes be derived.

One example of a system where this can be done is the following. There is a single service channel serving, in order of arrival, an unlimited queue fed by an input of identical units. The probability of an arrival and of a completion of service are alike independent both of time and of the state of the system. This requires mathematically a Poisson distribution of events and a distribution of the intervals between events which is exponential.

In respect of arrivals, the average rate of arrival in unit time is denoted by λ. Hence the probability of one arrival in the interval of time dt is given by λdt, and the probability of no arrivals in time dt as $1 - \lambda dt$.

In respect of servicing, the average service time is denoted by $1/\mu$. Hence the probability of completing the servicing of one unit in the interval of time dt is μdt, and the probability of no completions of service as $1 - \mu dt$.

What the decision-maker is particularly interested in is the probability of there being any given number in the system at any particular time, and what is the probability of an arrival having to wait for service. Mathematical expressions for these can be derived.

Let the probability that there are n units in the system be denoted by $P(n,t)$. This includes any already being served.

The probability that there are $n-1$ units in the system at time $t+dt$ is made up of:

first, the probability that there were $n-1$ units in the system at time t and that there were no arrivals and no completions of service in the interval dt; together with

secondly, the probability that there were n units in the system at time t, that one of these completed its service in the interval of time dt and that there were no arrivals in that interval; together with

thirdly, the probability that there were $n-2$ units in the system, that there was an arrival of one unit in the interval of time dt and that there were no completions of service in that interval; together with

fourthly, the probability of there being movements in and out of the system greater than one unit in the interval of time.

The first probability is expressed as $P(n-1,t)(1-\lambda dt)(1-\mu dt)$

The second probability is expressed as $P(n,t)(1-\lambda dt)\mu dt$

The third probability is expressed as $P(n-2,t)\lambda dt(1-\mu dt)$

All probabilities in the fourth category involve terms of the order of dt^2. Ignoring all terms in dt^2, and assuming n is greater than 1 so that $n-1$ is greater than 0,

$$P(n-1,t+dt) = P(n-1,t)(1-\lambda dt-\mu dt)+P(n,t)\mu dt+P(n-2,t)\lambda dt$$

This can be rearranged to read

$$\frac{P(n-1,t+dt)-P(n-1,t)}{dt} = -(\lambda+\mu)P(n-1,t)+\mu P(n,t)+\lambda P(n-2,t)$$

In the limit when $dt \to 0$, this becomes

$$\frac{dP(n-1,t)}{dt} = -(\lambda+\mu)P(n-1,t)+\mu P(n,t)+\lambda P(n-2,t)$$

It can also be shown that when $n = 1$

$$\frac{dP(0,t)}{dt} = -\lambda P(0,t)+\mu P(1,t)$$

Provided that μ is greater than λ, the state of the system will tend towards one in which the probabilities are independent of time and hence

$$\frac{dP(n-1,t)}{dt} = 0$$

and

$$\frac{dP(0,t)}{dt} = 0.$$

The equations therefore become

$$\mu P(n) = (\lambda+\mu)P(n-1) - \lambda P(n-2)$$
$$\mu P(1) = \lambda P(0)$$

From this it can be deduced that the probability of n units in this steady state system is given by

$$P_n = \rho^n(1-\rho)$$

where $\rho = \lambda/\mu$, and that the average number of units in the system is given by

$$\frac{\rho}{1-\rho}$$

and that the number of units in the queue (i.e. excluding those already in the servicing channel) is given by

$$\frac{\rho^2}{1-\rho}$$

A unit joining the system will have to wait from time t to time $t+dt$ for service if, of n units in the system when it arrives, $n-1$ completions are made in time t and the nth completion is in the interval t to $t+dt$. Thus the probability that this unit will have to wait during this interval is given by the product of these two probabilities multiplied by the probability of there being n units in the system when this unit arrives.

The completions of service form a Poisson distribution. Hence the probability of $n-1$ completions in time t is

$$\frac{(\mu t)^{n-1}e^{-\mu t}}{(n-1)!}$$

The probability of n units being in the system when one arrives is $\rho^n/(1-\rho)$. The probability of one completion in the interval t to $t+dt$ is μdt. Thus the probability that the unit will have to wait in time t to $t+dt$ is

$$\frac{\rho^n(1-\rho)(\mu t)^{n-1}e^{-\mu t}\mu dt}{(n-1)!}$$

To obtain the total probability of a unit requiring to wait, the individual probabilities for each value of n from one to infinity have to be considered. The sum of these is what is required. This is

$$\rho(\mu - \lambda)e^{-t(\mu - \lambda)}$$

where $\rho = \lambda/\mu$.

From this it can be deduced that the average waiting time of a unit is given by

$$\frac{\rho}{\mu(1-\rho)} \text{ or } \frac{\rho}{\mu - \lambda}$$

as in the section on waiting time problems in Chapter 2.

LOGICAL DEDUCTION

THE application of logic to problem-solving proceeds by successive steps of reasoning from the statement of a premiss or set of premisses to the reaching of a solution.

The statement of the premisses in its widest terms comprises:

(a) the inclusion of certain facts as relevant;
(b) the acceptance of certain opinions as valid;
(c) the making of certain assumptions.

Given that the problem is correctly specified in this way, reaching the conclusion is an automatic process.

Consider the following pieces of information.

1 There are five houses in a street
2 White lives in 'Woodburn'
3 Black owns a dog
4 The car at 'Oak Bank' is a Vauxhall
5 Green owns an Austin
6 'Oak Bank' is immediately to the right of 'Westleigh' from the observers' view
7 Susan owns a guinea-pig
8 Mary lives in 'Tevesnol'
9 The car at the middle house is a Humber
10 Brown lives in the first house
11 Jackie lives next door to the house where there is a cat
12 Mary lives next door to where a horse is kept
13 Melanie has a Rolls Royce
14 Smith's wife is called Mona
15 Brown lives next door to 'Iona'

From this information it is required to find

(a) Who owns a Ford?
(b) Who keeps goldfish?

Before attempting to find the solution, it is necessary first to observe that the pieces of information made available do not completely specify the problem. They represent the facts and opinions that are to be included but, before a solution can be found, certain assumptions must also be made. The nature of the assumptions will determine the solution.

1 It must be assumed that there *is* somebody who owns a Ford.
2 Equally it must be assumed that somebody *does* keep goldfish.
3 An assumption must be made as to the definition of the word 'first'. In the western world this would be 'on the extreme left from the observer's view'. It must also be accepted that 1, 2, 3, 4, 5 is the correct sequence of numbers.
4 The relationships of the five characteristics in each of the five sets must be considered. These characteristics are:

    (*a*) the householder's name
    (*b*) the name of the house
    (*c*) the make of car
    (*d*) the wife's name
    (*e*) the pet in the house.

Various assumptions could be made. One such, which will be followed here in finding a solution, is that there is one and one only of each of the characteristics in each set.

These assumptions made, the reasoning can proceed. It is convenient to display the results of the argument in tabular form, using a framework as shown, into which conclusions can be inserted. In the argument that follows, the numbers in brackets refer to the pieces of information given.

	1	2	3	4	5
Householder's name					
Name of house					
Make of car					
Wife's name					
Type of pet					

There are certain pieces of information, taken along with the assumptions, which lead to unique conclusions. Thus (10) Brown lives in the first house, taken with the assumption as to the definition of 'first', identifies Brown as living in No. 1. Equally (9) identifies the car at No. 3 as a Humber. (15) identifies the house name of No. 2 as 'Iona'. Inserting these, the display panel becomes

	1	2	3	4	5
Householder's name	Brown				
Name of house		Iona			
Make of car			Humber		
Wife's name					
Type of pet					

This seems, at first glance, to exhaust the unique conclusions, but this is not so. (6) leads to the conclusion that 'Oak Bank' and 'Westleigh' cannot be either No. 1 or No. 2, and (2) to the conclusion that 'Woodburn' cannot be either No. 1 or No. 2. No. 2 is already identified as 'Iona' and therefore, remembering the fourth assumption, the house name of No. 1 is identified as 'Tevesnol'. (8) then places Mary in No. 1, and (12) places the horse at No. 2. The display panel now becomes

	1	2	3	4	5
Householder's name	Brown				
Name of house	Tevesnol	Iona			
Make of car			Humber		
Wife's name	Mary				
Type of pet		Horse			

This position in the argument can be represented on a form of decision tree as node A (Figure 27).

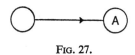

Fig. 27.

Now, however, two choices are available for further progress.

Either No. 3, No. 4 and No. 5 are 'Woodburn', 'Westleigh' and 'Oak Bank' respectively,

Or No. 3, No. 4 and No. 5 are 'Westleigh', 'Oak Bank' and 'Woodburn' respectively.

These two possibilities are shown on the decision tree as follows (Figure 28).

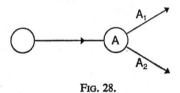

FIG. 28.

Display panels A_1 and A_2 show the position reached at the open end of arrows A_1 and A_2 respectively.

A_1	1	2	3	4	5
Householder's name	Brown				
Name of house	Tevesnol	Iona	Woodburn	Westleigh	Oak Bank
Make of car			Humber		
Wife's name	Mary				
Type of pet		Horse			

A_2	1	2	3	4	5
Householder's name	Brown				
Name of house	Tevesnol	Iona	Westleigh	Oak Bank	Woodburn
Make of car			Humber		
Wife's name	Mary				
Type of pet		Horse			

Two further steps can now be taken, and these must be taken along *both* A_1 and A_2. (2) identifies White as living at No. 3 in A_1, and at No. 5 in A_2. (4) also leads to a positive insertion in each display panel. These are now

A_1	1	2	3	4	5
Householder's name	Brown		White		
Name of house	Tevesnol	Iona	Woodburn	Westleigh	Oak Bank
Make of car			Humber		Vauxhall
Wife's name	Mary				
Type of pet		Horse			

A_2	1	2	3	4	5
Householder's name	Brown				White
Name of house	Tevesnol	Iona	Westleigh	Oak Bank	Woodburn
Make of car			Humber	Vauxhall	
Wife's name	Mary				
Type of pet		Horse			

None of the remaining pieces of information leads to unique deductions, and so the display panels represent two further nodes on the Decision Tree (Figure 29).

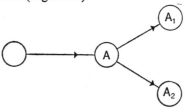

FIG. 29.

The residences of Black, Green and Smith have not yet been identified. Considering A_1 for the moment,

    (3) tells us that Black may live at No. 4 or No. 5
    (5) tells us that Green may live at No. 2 or No. 4
    (14) tells us that Smith may live at No. 2, No. 4 or No. 5.

There are three ways, and only three ways, in which these can all be true. These are:

1 Smith at No. 2	2 Smith at No. 4	3 Smith at No. 5
Green at No. 4	Green at No. 2	Green at No. 2
Black at No. 5	Black at No. 5	Black at No. 4

When A_2 is inspected, it is seen that the possibilities are:

1 Smith at No. 4   2 Smith at No. 3
  Green at No. 2   Green at No. 2
  Black at No. 3   Black at No. 4

Three arrows therefore emerge from A_1 and two from A_2 (Figure 30).

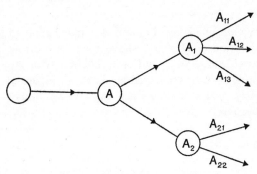

FIG. 30.

When the conclusions from (3), (5) and (14) have been inserted, five display panels can be constructed. These are A_{11}, A_{12}, A_{13}, A_{21}, A_{22}. The panels for A_{11}, A_{13}, and A_{21} are as follows:

A_{11}	1	2	3	4	5
Householder's name	Brown	Smith	White	Green	Black
Name of house	Tevesnol	Iona	Woodburn	Westleigh	Oak Bank
Make of car			Humber	Austin	Vauxhall
Wife's name	Mary	Mona			
Type of pet		Horse			Dog

A_{13}	1	2	3	4	5
Householder's name	Brown	Green	White	Black	Smith
Name of house	Tevesnol	Iona	Woodburn	Westleigh	Oak Bank
Make of car		Austin	Humber		Vauxhall
Wife's name	Mary				Mona
Type of pet		Horse		Dog	

A_{21}	1	2	3	4	5
Householder's name	Brown	Green	Black	Smith	White
Name of house	Tevesnol	Iona	Westleigh	Oak Bank	Woodburn
Make of car		Austin	Humber	Vauxhall	
Wife's name	Mary			Mona	
Type of pet		Horse	Dog		

The construction of panels A_{12} and A_{22} may be left to the reader.

A consideration of (13) now shows that the information in it is compatible with A_{13}, A_{21} and A_{22}, but not with A_{11} and A_{12}, which can therefore be truncated as shown in Figure 31.

The display panels for the open extreme positions of A_{13} and A_{21} now become

A_{13}	1	2	3	4	5
Householder's name	Brown	Green	White	Black	Smith
Name of house	Tevesnol	Iona	Woodburn	Westleigh	Oak Bank
Make of car		Austin	Humber	Rolls-Royce	Vauxhall
Wife's name	Mary			Melanie	Mona
Type of pet		Horse		Dog	

A_{21}	1	2	3	4	5
Householder's name	Brown	Green	Black	Smith	White
Name of house	Tevesnol	Iona	Westleigh	Oak Bank	Woodburn
Make of car		Austin	Humber	Vauxhall	Rolls-Royce
Wife's name	Mary			Mona	Melanie
Type of pet		Horse	Dog		

A consideration of (7) now shows that A_{21} and A_{22} must be truncated, leaving A_{13} as the only open arrow. A consideration of (11), taking account of assumption 4, leads to the final position as illustrated in Figure 32.

The display panel is

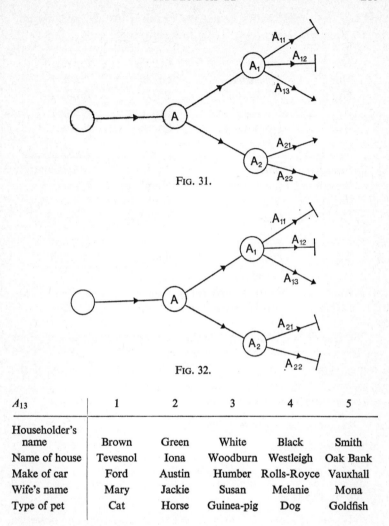

Fig. 31.

Fig. 32.

A_{13}	1	2	3	4	5
Householder's name	Brown	Green	White	Black	Smith
Name of house	Tevesnol	Iona	Woodburn	Westleigh	Oak Bank
Make of car	Ford	Austin	Humber	Rolls-Royce	Vauxhall
Wife's name	Mary	Jackie	Susan	Melanie	Mona
Type of pet	Cat	Horse	Guinea-pig	Dog	Goldfish

The final conclusions then are that

1 The Ford is owned by Brown
2 The goldfish are kept by Smith.

The preparation of a marketing plan, given as an example of a problem of analysis in Chapter III, will be recognized as similar to the problem solved in this appendix. It is, however, more than similar—it is an identical problem. Indeed, the problem in Chapter

o

III was prepared by translating the problem in the appendix into marketing terms according to the following code.

No. 1	*Luxury*	Brown	*Product C*
No. 2	*Expensive*	Green	*Product E*
No. 3	*Moderate*	White	*Product A*
No. 4	*Normal*	Black	*Product D*
No. 5	*Inexpensive*	Smith	*Product B*

Tevesnol	*Yellow*	Ford	*Older women*
Iona	*Blue*	Austin	*Middle class*
Woodburn	*Red*	Humber	*Teenagers*
Westleigh	*Black*	Rolls-Royce	*Lower Class*
Oak Bank	*Green*	Vauxhall	*Housewives*

Mary	*Hoarding*	Cat	£20,000
Jackie	*Cinema*	Horse	£15,000
Susan	*Television*	Guinea-pig	£10,000
Melanie	*Daily newspapers*	Dog	£5,000
Mona	*Weekly periodicals*	Goldfish	£3,000

If this code is used to translate the facts, opinions and assumptions of the problem into marketing terms, it will be found that, with minor exceptions in modes of expression, the specification of the problem in Chapter III emerges.

There are five houses in a street

> becomes *There are five products*

White lives in Woodburn

> becomes *Product A is to be red*

Black owns a dog

> becomes *Product D is to be given* £5,000 *advertising appropriation*

and so on.

The assumption that the order of houses requires No. 1 to be on the left from the viewer's point of view, and that 1, 2, 3, 4 and 5 are in sequence, translates into the assumption that the products can be arranged in the price range order luxury, expensive, moderate, normal and inexpensive. Hence, a marketing plan can be obtained by translating the solution in this appendix into marketing terms as follows:

Price range	Luxury	Expensive	Moderate	Normal	Inexpensive
Product	C	E	A	D	B
Colour	Yellow	Blue	Red	Black	Green
Customer class	Older women	Middle class	Teenage girls	Lower class	Housewives
Advertising medium	Hoardings	Cinema	Television	Daily newspapers	Weekly periodicals
Appropriation	£20,000	£15,000	£10,000	£5,000	£3,000

The steps in the analysis can follow a different sequence. Whether the full analysis is done depends on the form of the questions to which answers are required. If they are specific questions of details, and it is known that there is only a single answer to each, then as soon as these are found the analysis can be suspended.

If the analysis is to find a complete general solution, as in the case of the marketing plan, and any solution is acceptable, then as soon as one is found the analysis can be suspended. In this case, of course, straight-forward trial and error methods may also reveal an acceptable solution.

If, however, all possible solutions are required, then the full analysis must be done, and a trial and error method would require the examination of every conceivable pattern. If in this case one of the possible solutions and one only is to be selected, the specification of the problem must include a criterion of choice by which the acceptable solutions are to be judged.

The method by which the analysis proceeds is quite independent of the background of the problem. The method requires the use of logical deductive principles only, which are applicable to any of the problems whatever their backgrounds. In reality, the problems are all the same problem and, if they were stated in mathematical terms using symbols, one specification would suffice.

Where specialist expertise is required is in the specification of the problem. Judgement is needed to decide

1 what facts are relevant;
2 what opinions are valid;
3 what assumptions are reasonable;
4 what criterion is to be used for choosing from a number of acceptable solutions.

This done, the process of finding the solution is an automatic process, to be carried out by one skilled in the arts of reasoning, or in the ultimate to be programmed for a computer.

As always, the responsibility of the numerate manager is not lessened, but its direction of application is changed and the time when it is exercised is brought forward.

BIBLIOGRAPHY

The following books are suggested for further reading.

General

BEER, Stafford, *Cybernetics and Management*, English Universities Press, 1959.

BEER, Stafford, *Decision and Control: the Meaning of Operational Research*, Wiley, 1966.

CHERRY, C., *On Human Communication*, Wiley: Chapman & Hall, 1957.

DIEBOLD, J., *Beyond Automation: Managerial Problems of an Exploding Technology*, McGraw-Hill, 1964.

DRUCKER, P. F., *Managing for Results*, Heinemann, 1964.

DUCKWORTH, W. E., *A Guide to Operational Research*, 2nd edition, Methuen, 1964.

HILTON, Alice Mary, *Logic, Computing Machines and Automation*, Spartan Books (Washington), 1963.

RIVETT, B. H. P. and ACKOFF, R. L., *A Manager's Guide to Operational Research*, Wiley, 1963.

SARGEAUNT, M. J., *Operational Research for Management*, Heinemann, 1965.

STEWART, Rosemary, *The Reality of Management*, Heinemann, 1963.

WILLIAMS, J. D., *The Complete Strategyst*, Revised edition, McGraw-Hill, 1965.

Techniques

BATTERSBY, A., *A Guide to Stock Control*, Pitman, 1962.

BATTERSBY, A., *Mathematics in Management*, Penguin Books, 1966.

BATTERSBY, A., *Network Analysis for Planning and Scheduling*, 2nd edition, Macmillan, 1967.

BELLMAN, R. E. and DREYFUS, S., *Applied Dynamic Programming*, Princeton University, 1962.

CHURCHMAN, C. W. *et al.*, *Introduction to Operations Research*, Wiley, 1959.

FLETCHER, A. and CLARKE, G., *Management and Mathematics*, Business Publications, 1964.

HOULDON, B. T., *Some Techniques of Operational Research*, English Universities Press, 1962.

LOCKYER, K., *An Introduction to Critical Path Analysis*, 2nd edition, Pitman, 1967.

MAKOWER, M. S. and WILLIAMSON, E., *Teach Yourself Operational Research*, English Universities Press, 1967.

MORSE, P. M., *Queues, Inventories and Maintenance*, Wiley: Chapman & Hall, 1958.

TOCHER, K. D., *The Art of Simulation*, Van Nostrand, 1963.

VAJDA, S., *Mathematical Programming*, Addison-Wesley Publishing Co., 1961.

VAJDA, S., *Readings in Linear Programming*, Pitman, 1958.

VAJDA, S., *The Theory of Games and Linear Programming*, Wiley, 1956, Reprinted Methuen, 1963.

VON NEUMANN, J. and MORGENSTERN, O., *Theory of Games and Economic Behavior*, 3rd edition, Science Editions Inc., 1964.

Statistical Techniques

BROWN, R. G., *Smoothing, Forecasting and Prediction of Discrete Time Series*, Prentice Hall, 1963.

GOODMAN, R., *Teach Yourself Statistics*, English Universities Press, 1957.

MORONEY, M. J., *Facts from Figures*, 3rd edition, Penguin Books, 1956.

Automation

ASHBY, W. ROSS, *Introduction to Cybernetics*, University Paperbacks, 1964.

BOWDEN, B. V., *Faster than Thought*, Pitman, 1953.

BURTON, A. J. and MILLS, R. G., *Electronic Computers and their Business Applications*, Ernest Benn, 1960.

WESTWATER, F. L., *Teach Yourself Electronic Computers*, English Universities Press, 1962.

Included in this glossary are those terms, not necessarily all occurring in the text, which will be encountered by the numerate manager in discussions with his experts.

Apart from a few basic general definitions, the terms are classified as follows:

Computer terms: those relating to the equipment included in computing systems.

Computer operating terms: those relating to the operation of computing systems.

Mathematical terms: those relating to methods of evaluation and logical deduction where choice is either not involved or has already been made.

Statistical terms: those concerning measurement.

Operational research terms: those relating to methods of evaluation and logical deduction where choice is involved.

Access. A computer operating term: making contact with a memory unit so that information can be obtained from or placed into storage.

Address. A computer operating term: a means of identifying the location of data in storage or its source or its destination. The identification is generally represented by a number, a label or a name.

Algol. A computer operating term: an abbreviation for algorithmic orientated language.

Algorithm. A mathematical term: a computational process or procedure in which a desired result can be effectively obtained from various initial data.

Alphanumeric. A computer operating term: a contraction of alphabetical-numerical, which describes data containing both alphabetical and numerical elements.

Arithmetic Instruction. A computer operating term: an instruction in a program which causes the computer to perform an arithmetic operation.

Arithmetic Unit. A computer term: the unit in an electronic computing system which contains the circuits that perform arithmetic operations.

Assemble. A computer operating term: to prepare a machine language program from a symbolic language program.

Automation. The performance of processes of operation and control by automatic means.

Auxiliary Storage. A computer term: means of storing data elsewhere than in the main store of a computer.

Bi-modal. A statistical term: descriptive of a series of observations where there are two modes (*q.v.*).

Binary. A mathematical term: descriptive of a system of representing numbers with a base of two, in contrast to the decimal system which uses a base of ten.

Binary Coded Decimal. A mathematical term: descriptive of a system of representing numbers in which *each* digit of a decimal number is transformed into a binary code group.

Bit. A computer operating term: an abbreviation of binary digit, representing an elementary unit of information stored by a single electronic component.

Buffer. A computer term: a means of storing data in order to compensate for differences in the rates of flow of data in different parts of a data transmitting system.

Calculator. A computer term: a device capable of performing arithmetic.

Card Field. A computer operating term: a set of columns on a card which are identifiable by their position.

Channel. A computer term: a path along which signals can be sent.

Character. A computer operating term: one of a set of defined symbols.

Character Reader. A computer term: a device which can convert data represented in certain conventional scripts or typescripts on documents into a form suitable for input into computers.

Cobol. A computer operating term: an abbreviation for common business orientated language.

Code. A computer operating term: a set of rules or instructions.

Coder. A computer operating term: a person who prepares computer program instruction sequences from flow charts or algorithms.

Co-efficient of correlation. A statistical term: a measure of the strength of a mutual relationship, if one exists, between two variables.

Compiler. A computer operating term: a program that prepares in a machine language suitable for a particular computer a program written in a language suitable for another different computer.

Continuous Variable. A mathematical term: a quantity which is capable of taking any numerical value within a defined range.

Control Unit. A computer term: that part of a computing system which effects the retrieval and interpretation of the instructions of a program in their proper sequence and directs signals to the appropriate parts of the system in accordance with the interpretation.

Core Store. A computer term: a storage device consisting of an array of magnetic material in which the direction of magnetization in each unit is used to represent binary data.

Correlation. A statistical term: the relationship that exists between the movements of two varying quantities.

Critical Path Method. An operational research term: a technique using a network form of display to show inter-relationships between the elements of projects being planned.

Cybernetics. The science of control of sets of activities and relationships in man-machine systems and organizations.

Data Transmission. A computer operating term: the sending of data from one system to another system, or from one part of a system to another part of the same system.

Debug. A computer operating term: to detect, comprehend and remove mistakes from a program.

Decision Theory. An operational research term: a set of techniques for use in making decisions in conditions of uncertainty.

Decision Tree. An operational research term: a method of displaying the flow of possible courses of action in the form of a branching network.

Discounted Cash Flow. A mathematical term: a method of evaluating capital expenditure projects.

Disc Pack. A computer term: a storage device consisting of a set of discs of magnetic material on which data can be stored and from which it can be retrieved for processing.

Display Unit. A computer term: a device which provides a visual representation of data.

Error Detecting Code. A computer term: a code in which the representation of each piece of data is created according to specific rules so that transgressing of the rules enables errors to be detected automatically.

Executive Routine. A computer operating term: a program which in a computer with multi-access facilities controls the loading and relocation of routines being used.

Exponential Smoothing. A statistical term: a technique used in forecasting future values of observations being considered which gives progressively greater weight to more recent observations.

Field. A computer operating term: a specified area of a record of data.

File. A computer operating term: a collection of related records.

Flow Chart. A computer operating term: a graphical and symbolic representation of operations data flow and equipment included in the definition, analysis and solution of a problem.

Frequency Distribution. A statistical term: an arrangement of data giving the number of items of each category or the subject matter included in the observations.

Games Theory. An operational research term: a theory for the description and analysis of competitive situations to enable an optimum strategy to be selected to oppose an opponent who has a strategy of his own.

Hardware. A computer term: the physical equipment making up a computing system.

Heuristics. An operational research term: the theory of step-by-step discovery.

Histogram. A statistical term: a form of diagram in which the elements of a frequency distribution are represented by rectangles whose areas are proportional to the frequency of the observations.

Housekeeping Routine. A computer operating term: any process which must be performed to enable a machine run to proceed.

Information Processing. A computer operating term: taking in information, changing it and delivering the resulting information at the output.

Information Retrieval. A computer operating term: methods of recovering specific information from stored data.

Information System. A computer operating term: the network of communications within an organization.

Information Theory. The theory describing the recording, coding and transmission of information.

Input. A computer term: the data to be processed.

Input Unit. A computer term: equipment used to communicate data to a computer.

Inquiry Station. A computer term: a remote terminal device for interrogating data-processing equipment.

Instruction Time. A computer term: that part of an operating cycle during which the control unit is analysing the instruction and performing the indicated operation.

Interpreter Routine. A computer operating term: a routine that translates and executes a given program instruction expressed in any computer language not specific to the computer in use.

Interrupt. A computer operating term: to disrupt temporarily the operation of a routine to enable some other task to be performed.

Label. A computer operating term: one or more characters used to identify an instruction or an item of data.

Language. A computer operating term: a system for representing and communicating information or data between different parts of man-machine systems.

Line Printer. A computer term: equipment capable of printing in a single operation a complete line of characters.

Linear Programming. An operational research term: a technique for finding an optimum value or set of values in certain kinds of problems involving many variables.

Location. A computer term: a position, identified by an address, in the main internal store capable of holding a group of characters.

Machine Instruction. A computer operating term: an instruction that a given computer can recognize and execute.

Magnetic Drum. A computer term: a storage device in which data can be stored by selective magnetization of portions of the curved surface of a cylinder.

Mark Sensing. A computer operating term: a means of detecting marks made by special pencil in special places on a card and translating them into punched holes.

Master File. A computer operating term: a file containing relatively permanent information.

Mathematical Model. An operational research term: a means of representing by an equation or set of equations the behaviour of a process or concept and expressing the relationships between the inputs and outputs of the system.

Mean. A statistical term: an arithmetic average.

Median. A statistical term: a position average being the central value of the variable when the values are ranged in order of magnitude.

Merge. A computer operating term: to combine items from two or more sequenced files into one similarly sequenced file.

Millisecond. One thousandth part of a second (10^{-3}s).

Microsecond. One millionth part of a second (10^{-6}s).

Mode. A statistical term: the value of that observation which occurs most frequently in a series of items.

Monitor. A computer operating term: to supervise and verify the correct operations of a program during its execution.

Monte Carlo Method. An operational research term: a particular method of simulation of use in solving some waiting time problems.

Multiprogramming. A computer operating term: ensuring the interleaved or simultaneous operating of two or more programs by a single computer.

Multiprocessor. A computer term: equipment with multiple arithmetic and logic units for simultaneous use.

Nanosecond. One billionth of a second (10^{-9}s).

Network Analysis. An operational research term: a group of techniques for exploring the elements and relationships of complex planning projects and recording them as a network.

Noise. A computer operating term: any unwanted signal.

Off-line. A computer operating term: describes devices not in direct communication with the central unit of a computer.

On-line. A computer operating term: describes devices in direct communication with the central unit of a computer.

Operational Research. The use of a scientific approach and analytic methods for solving operational problems.

Parameter. A mathematical term: a variable not included in the description of a system, which in any particular case being considered is constant but in different cases could vary.

Pert. An operational research term: an abbreviation of program evaluation review technique, is one of the group of network analysis methods.

Population. A statistical term: the whole of the material from which a sample is taken. Is synonymous with universe.

Probability Theory. A statistical term: methods of using measures of likelihood of occurrence of chance events to predict the behaviour of a group.

Program Library. A computer operating term: a collection of available computer programs and routines.

Programming Language. A computer operating term: a language in which computer programs are written.

Queueing Theory. An operational research term: a form of probability theory used in studying certain waiting time problems.

Quota Sampling. A statistical term: a method of selection by which the sample is divided into quotas which indicate the number of people of a particular type to be interviewed, the choice of the actual interviewee being left to the interviewer.

Random Access. A computer operating term: the process of obtaining information from or placing information in storage in such a way that the time required for access is independent of the location of the information most recently handled.

Random Sampling. A statistical term: a method of selection in which every unit of a population has exactly the same chance of being included in the sample as any other unit.

Real Time. A computer operating term: describes computation performed during the actual time that the related physical process is occurring.

Redundancy. A computer operating term: the presence of excess information to help communication despite interference in transmission.

Register. A computer term: a device capable of storing a specified amount of data.

Regression Analysis. A statistical term: a method of establishing a relationship between sets of data.

Routine. A computer operating term: a set of coded instructions arranged in proper sequence to direct a computer to perform a desired operation or sequence of operations.

Sampling Error. A statistical term: the difference between the estimate of a value as obtained from a sample of a universe and the actual value.

Scatter Diagram. A statistical term: a visual means of displaying a correlation between two variables.

Simulation. An operational research term: the representation of physical systems and phenomena by conceptual models.

Software. A computer operating term: the totality of programs and routines used to deploy the capabilities of computers.

Sort. A computer operating term: to arrange data according to rules based upon a key contained in the items of the data.

Standard Deviation. A statistical term: a measure of the dispersion of the values of a series of observations from their arithmetic mean.

Stochastic Process. An operational research term: a process in which chance governs the particular state of items or events but where the probabilities governing the chances conform to a pattern.

Storage Register. A computer operating term: a register in the main store of a computer.

Systems Analysis. A computer operating term: the examination of the procedures of an operation to determine its objectives and the best methods of attaining them.

Universe. A statistical term: the whole of the material from which a sample is taken. Is synonymous with population.

Update. A computer operating term: to put into place in a master file changes required by current information or transactions.

Variable. A mathematical term: a quantity which can present more than one numerical value according to circumstance.

Variance. A statistical term: the square of the value of the standard deviation.

Word. A computer operating term: an ordered set of characters treated as one unit by computer circuits.

Word Length. A computer operating term: the number of bits or other characters in a word.

Zone. A computer operating term: an allocated portion of internal storage.

INDEX